To Kathleen &
MARyAnaro

So precious.   Pat Gilliss

The Other Side of
Broken

By: Pat Gilliss

Cover designed by Pat Gilliss

Photography and art work by
Paige McIlvain

TGG Publishing Copyright c 2018

Email GlennPat77@gmail.com

ISBN-13: 978-1984238672

ISBN-10: 1984238671

Some names and situations have been changed to protect their privacy.

Contents

My Dedication

~~~~~~

I would like to dedicate this book to a precious young man named Landon. He was born twelve years ago, and there were complications during delivery. Because of the complications, his survival looked very bleak. He coded before the helicopter could fly him to the best equipped hospital, many miles away. At this time, they certainly were not offered much hope for his survival.

His grandparents immediately called their church prayer chain, and others to start praying for this little guy. Jesus heard those prayers and answered. Even though they were told the child would not survive, he still lives!

Landon, smiles all the day long; so cheerful, and happy even with the daily challenges he has at this time.

We ask for prayers of healing for our Landon. We believe Jesus can do anything. They told us Landon has quadriplegia with cerebral palsy. He does not speak. However, he now moves his legs!

I have taken this little guy on my heart and dedicate this book to him. We are asking each of you that read this, to pray for our Landon like he was your child. I believe God for this extraordinary miracle. I know my Lord can do this.

Please help us to bombard Heaven with prayers. Landon's pictures are in my book so you can see the sunshine he holds within his little heart. I thank you all for your sweet efforts. I know there are many prayer warriors out there! I promise you, they will be heard and considered by God.

I personally, thank you all.

Landon's Pictures

VII

Acknowledgments

~~~~~~~~~~~~~~~~~~~~~~~

First of all, I would like to thank the Lord for helping me every step of the way to make this book the best that I have to offer. If He was not in it with me, I could not do anything. In fact, it was His idea, not mine. I said after the first book, "You Asked GOD for What?!" "Never again!" After the second book, "No More Crumbs." I repeated it once more. But God had a different plan, and here I am on book number three. I don't think I shall predict what happens next. I will let Him lead me instead.

I would also thank all my friends for encouraging me to write another one. I can hardly believe I am doing this. But, "I can do all things through Christ who strengthens me." Philippians 4:13

My hat is off to all of you, who have helped me so much with correcting. May God bless each one of you for all YOU have done to help me look good!

Pamala Carr, we had to do it by email but you sure did it! You are such an amazing woman, and a very dear friend. You are more like my little buddy, and confident.

Janice Knox, your teaching abilities really came in handy with my run on sentences! You were such a great help, and such a dear sweet lady to work with.

Cathy Kohland, I named you hawk eye! We both chuckled, but you were the proof reader that found the tiny things. You did a great job.

JoAnn McIlvain, Chief Editor, you are so talented it's hard to believe we came from the same womb! You are so organized, and I'm so not! You are an amazing Editor. I have no doubt this book would not have been what I hoped and prayed it would be. Without your very strong and loving touch, it could never have been produced.

It seemed that God had each one of you zero in on something different to watch for, and what a great team you made! Truly, I cannot thank you enough. God has blessed me with the best loving team I could have ever had!

Glenn Gilliss has remained my logistics man, and scriptural researcher. You are my prayer partner, encourager, and inspiration. While writing these stories, during the time of dealing with hard emotions, you were my shoulder to cry on. You are still rock steady in all you do. God sent you to me as my very special blessing. Thank you so much for all you do to help me. Jesus truly handpicked you for me, and I love you.

Pastor and Sister Andrus, You are always my leading angels of light! You are always ready to help teach the good Word of God. Through crisis, or happy times, you were always there. Had you not set all of your personal plans aside, and moved to Milford, my life would have been very different. Never under estimate what you have done for God. He has books full of the kindness and goodness you have shown to all of those in His kingdom. I will love you forever. I remember, Sister Andrus, at a ladies meeting one night, you pointed to me and said, "Sister Patty Gilliss, you have a book inside of you that needs to be written." I smiled and thought, "That's not going to happen"! But, you were right. This is my third one! Your love has motivated many things in my life. I thank you.

Paige McIlvain, you took a picture from my phone, and made it look so professional! I love, love, love the new cover you have made out of my mistake! You are really good, girl! It says everything I wanted it to say.

I always pray God's blessing can be felt so strong on the cover, it will make people want to reach out and touch it. Once again, you made it look beautiful. I could not have done this without you. As if that wasn't enough, you uploaded the book for me, and it turned out great! I loved you before all of this, but I want you to know, how grateful I am. Thank you! Thank you!

Last, but not least, I want to thank my children. You have lived through many of these stories with me. Mom and Dad are so proud of the great adults you have all become. What a wonderful peace it is, for a parent to know you each married well. You are working hard and making your way through life. Because you have lived preaching, teaching, and helping others find their way along life's paths, you have made the world a better place.

Wayne and Paula Gilliss, Tim and Amy Plump, Steve and Ashley Malandrino, Andrew and Charity Gilliss, Mom and Dad love you all dearly. We are so blessed you were born to us.

Finally, thanks to all of those who allowed me to share your stories. Because of your kind gesture, others may come to believe. I could not have done it without you! Allowing me to print them will help many others believe Jesus for anything, too. May God bless each one of you.

Preface

~~~~~~

I have written my heart in the pages of this book. As I have written and re·lived these trying and blessed times, I have cried tears of joy and tears of sorrow. I felt great happiness and terrible pain you could not imagine. But most of all I have felt God's healing.

I wrote this book to try to help many others deal with their pain and sorrow. I know there will be some of you who can't begin to understand such anguish. Others may know much worse than I have shared in my book. While I pray you haven't tasted of this bitter pill, I know without a doubt some of you have.

I asked Jesus to help me be able to deal with the memories, so you realize you are not alone. "Help me, Lord, to be able to touch others and lead them to YOU, the Healer! Help me to show them, through your love, happier days are coming and will stay with them forever."

I want to share with you the view from the eyes of a child. In this book, I have a tendency to categorize lifestyles for different people's lives. For example, my husband came up in a "Father Knows Best" type of home, and I grew up in a "Ma and Pa Kettle" situation. Many of you may be too young to remember these television shows produced during my childhood, but several of you will understand.

The one thing I remember is, an eleven year old girl knelt at a little church altar and met Jesus Christ for the very first time. After a few years, my Parents left that small church, and of course, I had to go with them. But I never forgot the touch He placed on my young life that day. Many years later, I found Him once again, and my life has never been the same.

Since then, I have had some hard times, but once I found Him the second time, I knew I would never leave Him again. I would not allow anyone to take the wonderful love, I have been blessed to find twice in my life, from me.

I hope you learn from my journey, and bring yourself to the place in Him, you will never want to leave again, either. I love living in His presence and we are the best of friends. This old world is winding down, and He is coming soon! I want to make it to that city where the Lamb is the Light. On my way out of this world, I want to take as many to Heaven with me as I can. I pray these stories will give you a hunger to live for Jesus like your life depends on it, because it does. Remember, only what's done for Christ will last.

What Goes Around Comes Around

~~~~~~

It was almost dark; the leaves were now dropping. It was a slow, steady, rainy, night in the fall. It was a miserable night to be out. The man I was married to at the time, was driving through Camden, Delaware. We had quite a significant amount of cash in the car from his business. As we were nearing the center of town, the traffic was very heavy; many were headed to the bank this Friday night, as were we, before it closed.

I usually didn't ride with him to the bank, but he was in a good mood for a change and asked me to ride along. While I was surprised he had asked me, I agreed.

As we were nearing our destination, I glanced out my side window and saw a tiny boy come out the side door of his house. The outside light allowed me to see he did not have a stitch of clothes on. He was running as fast as his little feet could carry him and heading straight for the street. Being a mother myself, I knew this was not supposed to be happening. I yelled, "Stop the car!" My husband slammed on the brakes and I jumped out of the car, running for this little boy! At this moment, I did not have time to explain anything. I simply took off running, as fast as I could. Mind you, I was a much faster runner back then than I am now.

Ahead of us, the traffic was flying around the corner towards us. At that time of night, I knew no one was looking for a naked baby in the street. I also knew if I didn't catch him, he would be killed! Of course, at that particular moment, all of this wasn't running through my mind. I only processed, "That kid is

1

going to run into the street! No one will see him!"

As I approached the child, I reached out, grabbed his arm, and snatched him up close to me. He was only one step away from the oncoming car. When the driver saw ME, he slammed on the brakes at the same time!

I pressed the child in close to me; I cupped his little bare bottom in my hand and headed for the sidewalk. Horns were blowing from both directions. It was total confusion for that few seconds, but it seemed to last forever.

It was at this moment, I heard a woman screaming, as she was coming out that same door. I knew that mother had just discovered her baby was gone. I rounded the corner of her house quickly so she could see me; I thought she was going to faint right there in her yard.

Immediately, she began to explain to me her five year old was watching the baby on his potty. She said, "I told her not to leave him for a minute!" She was sobbing. I advised her, "It may be better just to keep your doors locked next time. I caught him just before he ran out in front of the car." This woman could not thank me enough. She was so grateful her child was safe. She hugged me, thanking me over and over again. I remember speaking words of comfort to her. Happy he was okay, I headed back to the dragon, I knew would be waiting for me in the car. Walking back toward the car, I noticed he was now parked. As I approached the car, I could see him glaring at me through the windshield. While I knew what was coming, I was feeling good in my heart that I had done the right thing. Quite frankly, I didn't care at the moment how mad he was. The child was alive. I knew I had saved that baby's life, only God himself, knows why I was there at that particular minute.

I won't go into the tongue lashing I took when I got back in the car. I was reprimanded because, knowing there was cash in the car, I didn't take time to shut the door. By the time he finished with his tongue lashing, I had been made to feel terrible for making such a rash move.

In my mind I was screaming, "Did you even see what I just did?" I was accustomed to tuning out his scolding's many times before. So, I took that route, and only pretended with an occasional grunt, to listen to him the rest of the way home.

Even now in my heart, as I relive the episode, I know without a doubt in the second it would have taken me to shut the door, that baby would have been in front of the oncoming car. Even though I didn't have time to think about what would be said to me once I got back to my car, it was very much worth the scolding. I had been in the right place at the right time, and saved a baby's life!

Now, I will fast forward, approximately twenty years later. As they say, "A lot of water has gone over the dam." I am remarried to a wonderful, loving husband, and now I have become the mother of two year old twins, Ashley and Andrew, and our two teens, Wayne and Amy.

On this beautiful sunny day, Glenn and I were sitting on the front porch of our old Victorian home, happily watching our twin babies playing nearby, with Glenn's sister. Everyone, including her, seemed to be in high spirits.

*It was almost noon, on a Friday. Because
downtown streets were currently being blacktopped, to
get to the other side of town, the traffic had been re-
routed to go by our house. This made our corner a very,
very, busy intersection.*

*After an enjoyable time on the porch, we all
decided to go back into the house. I had the twins by
their hands, and since she was last, I asked my sister in
law to be sure she latched the storm door.*

*I can't say for sure why she did not listen to me.
However, since I was never her favorite person, her
attitude was, "I don't have to do anything you tell me to
do." At this time in our lives, this behavior was very
typical of her. Unfortunately, I hadn't noticed she was in
one of her disgruntled states of mind, and perhaps my
merely asking her to do something was the cause of her
foul mood. Whatever the reason, my instincts didn't pick
up on it. So, I assumed she had locked the door, as I had
kindly requested her to do.*

*We were sitting around the breakfast nook table,
drinking coffee and tea. Everyone* **seemed** *to be in such a
relaxed mood and we were enjoying each other's
company.*

*We casually chatted at the table for over a half
hour, suddenly my front doorbell rang. When I answered
the door, I saw a very pleasant looking woman, about
thirty -five years of age standing on my porch, with a
very stressful look on her face. Reaching to unlatch and
open the door, I realized it had never been locked at all!
Even at this moment, I was thankful Andy and Ashley
were in the family room with Amy, and I was happy
Andy had not discovered it had been left unlocked!*

Breathlessly, she began to say, "I am very sorry

4

*to bother you, Ma'am, but we found this little boy in the
middle of this busy street. He is not even old enough to
tell us his name. I thought if he was from this
neighborhood, maybe you would recognize him." As I
stepped around the doorway onto the front porch so I
could see past the large tree trunk blocking my view,
there was my Andy!*

*To keep from fainting myself, I just drew my
breath in and whispered his name.*

*The woman went on to tell me, she didn't have
time to park her car, before she grabbed him out of the
street. So, she just opened her door, picked him up, and
sat him on her seat until she could get her vehicle to the
curb. She was worried someone would think she was
kidnapping him!*

*Trust me, the thought that went through my mind
was, anyone could have picked him up the same way and
kept on going! I began to cry and thanked her for saving
my child's life! I told her I thought Andy was in the
family room with his older sister the entire time. He
knew how to open the storm door, but he didn't know
how to UNLOCK it. He was able to sneak out,
undetected, because my sister in law, neglected to do as I
had requested.*

*When I walked back into the breakfast nook, with
Andy in my arms, I began to tell the woman's story and
how she found him in the middle of the busy street. I am
sure, as angry as I was at that moment, smoke could be
seen flowing from my ears! GRRRR!*

*I must tell you; I was trying very hard to hold
myself together. I looked my sister in law right in
the eyes and said, "I asked you nicely, to latch that door!
Andy doesn't know how to unlock it!" I said it very*

curtly, and I meant it very curtly! I think because she knew in her heart, that she purposely did not lock the door...and WHY... there was nothing else to be said. She just got up and left the house, which at the moment, was probably the wisest thing she could have done. I am sure she did not realize he would slip out, but this could have been a horrible way for all of us to learn a valuable lesson!

After that day, I always locked the doors myself. You have to have experienced something like this to fully understand my anguish. In some cases, if you want it done right, you must do it yourself.

After everyone was gone and I had calmed down enough that even God could talk to my heart, He gently reminded me it was a payback. Then He began to take my mind way back to that rainy night, and the baby that I had saved twenty years previously.

He spoke to me, "That which you sow, ye shall surely reap." .... Galatians 6:7 They say it differently nowadays; "What goes around comes around." But, He who is faithful does not forget.

He saw me twenty years before, and He saw my child that day. Even though twenty years ago I was not living for Him, He STILL saw what I had done. He let me know He had remembered, and today, He was blessing me back. Even now, reliving this memory makes tears sting my eyes pondering the what if's.

That adorable baby has grown up to be a God loving man, and a great husband. He works in the law enforcement field, plays percussion in church, and lives a full life, because God spared him. I love the benefits of living for God. They never get old or boring. I was delighted in this case that, "What goes around did *indeed come around." During my lifetime, Jesus has been so good to me. I cannot tell it all!*

I want to mention, that same sister -in- love, gave her heart to God, and was baptized in the name of Jesus. It was wonderful. We had been praying for her salvation for years. While we had our moments, our prayers were always for her salvation.

When she passed on to a higher place, she was happy to go on with Him. Her Mother and Dad were there waiting for her. All the pain she had suffered in life was now ended.

It was such a comfort for Glenn and me to know, she made it to that city, where the Lamb is the Light. One day soon, we will see her again,

*Remember, when you do something kind for someone, God writes it all down, He remembers **all** the good we do; and when we ask, He forgives all the bad, and remembers it no more.*

God is so good! He was good to me yesterday, He has blessed me today, and He will take care of me forever!

The Terrible Waste
of Unused Authority

~~~~~~

*I will start this story out by saying, in my forty -
three plus years of living for God, I have learned many
interesting things. I have learned the devil is NOT,
omnipresent, even though he would like us to believe he
is. He would also like us to think, if God opens a door for
us, he is able to close it. This is also a lie. So, if he tells
you these things, remember there is no truth in him, and
unbelief is a crippling factor, that we shouldn't
entertain!*

*I have heard some people say it is boring to live a
Christian life, and I have heard many say it is
fascinating to live for God in these last days. I have
tasted of both opinions. I have become bored at times,
but soon realized that it was my own fault. The fact is,
we have been brought up in a world where we expect
others to help fill the voids in our lives. I was no
different. I am human.*

*My sister, JoAnn McIlvain, Christian Author of
"Drops In My Bucket," taught a lesson at a ladies tea we
held at our church, which was so inspiring. It was about
the many different hats, as women, we were expected to
wear in one day. I have worn many hats in life, and yes,
all in the same day. All together they make up my total
being. The times I chose to wear all of the easy hats, life
became boring. Yet, if I wore the work hard, nonstop
hats, daily life became overwhelming! But when I added
a bit of fun, and mixed it with trust and faith, they*

8

*seemed to balance together, and my world became an
actual wonderland. I have learned it is incredible what
God can do.*

Please read on.

~~~~~~

    *I want to start this story out with the fact that, in
myself, I am nothing! ZIP! If there is anything good in
me, it only comes from God. My flesh tries to rule most
of the time and often wins out. Still, there are times God
uses me. I don't know why, because I am full of flaws;
but I'm glad He does.*

    *In church one Sunday, God spoke this title to my
heart. It was a lesson He wanted me to share. I knew it
was His voice, because when He spoke the words, it
astounded me. I was halfway through this third book,
and I had been praying for Him to give me some lesson
type stories to include in this book, as He had done in
the first two.*

    *As I began to ponder this title, He quickened to
my mind, "The Terrible Waste of Unused Authority".
Immediately, I could feel His presence. So many
thoughts flooded my mind and heart. I really should
have written down more than I did at that time to help
me remember it all. However, I was in the Sunday
School class and didn't want to appear as though I
wasn't listening. I always sit close to the front, to avoid
getting distracted from the teacher.*

    *I began to think about what actual authority
meant, and I realized there are several facets that come
with authority. Yes, it gives us power to accomplish
many things, but it also causes us to give respect to
those who have it. For example, my Pastor receives a*

great deal of respect from many people. He has never
demanded it and never asked me for it. Yet, I respect
him highly because of who he is, who he represents, and
the life he and his precious family live before me.
Another example is Police Officers. I have never been
asked one time by any Police Officer to give them my
respect. However, I genuinely do. Why? Because I know
they would put their own lives in danger to protect mine.
This thought alone, makes me want to respect them. I
think you get the picture.

We must also realize that only a higher authority
can designate authority. You can't purchase God's
authority like some people purchase it in the political
field. (Not that they all do, but we won't go there.) I am
speaking of God given authority.

We, as Christians, give the enemy of our soul way
too much confidence. This past couple of years, Jesus has
been dealing with me on this subject. I don't know how I
let the enemy trick me into these kinds of thoughts, and
I am ashamed to admit he does. I have learned if anyone
is going to be miserable, it's not going to be me! Jesus
has given me permission to **Rock hell** with my spoken
words, and wreak havoc, in the enemies' kingdom.

We, as His children, have been given authority
over the principality of the air and darkness. Whoa! We
have been given the power to tread on serpents; this
does not mean we should go out and step on snakes! NO!
This power says, if we accidentally step on one, we can
use the authority He gave to us, as Paul did. There was
no other help to be found, he had to shake it off in the
fire, and trust in God! Serpents may also be a
representation of spiritual wickedness. Keep in mind, all
snakes do not crawl on the ground outside. Through

prayer, we have the power to shake this kind of spiritual serpent off, too.

*As HIS children, we **have** authority to call on the mighty Name of Jesus and rebuke the devil, sickness, fear, and any evilness around us. It is written in His word; "He gives us **power** (authority) over ALL,.... **the power of the enemy....**" (Luke 10:19) In the next verse, it basically says, (Paraphrasing,) Don't let this fact go to your head!*

Jesus even spoke to the storms and sea waves, and they listened to Him. He cast out devils, and they left. Jesus spoke to a tree that was not producing to dry up and it did. He spoke to the sickness of a child miles away from where He was standing. Even from that distance, the child was healed! How did Jesus do this? He merely spoke it in faith, and the power of God that dwelt within Him, performed the miracle. Through the power of the spoken word, this was made possible.

*Now if you will notice, He did not just **think** these things. He spoke the words out loud, even to Satan. He said, Matthew 4:10 "Get thee hence, Satan!..." Why? because the devil was aggravating Him.*

Whenever I have heard preachers talk about this very subject, I have always wondered about something. After Jesus had fasted forty days in the wilderness, WHY would Satan even try to tempt Him? Surely, he knew who Jesus was! However, the devil also knew Jesus was weak in His flesh from fasting. I asked God, to please help me to understand.

*Right then, the thought came to my mind. Yes, the devil did know who Jesus was, and how much power He had; but the enemy was hoping, and testing Jesus, himself, that perhaps **He** didn't realize **His*** own omnipotent authority! But Jesus WAS secure in His God given authority. He knew without a doubt, just how much He carried within Him at all times. He rebuked the devil and made him flee. Now, I think you get the picture of what one can do with spiritual authority. Let's bring it down to the level of our everyday living.

God has been dealing with me concerning this scripture for years "....Greater works, shall ye do...." John: 14:12 He spoke it not just **to** us, but "into" us.

I am sure Jesus meant, as far as greater signs and wonders go, they will never be greater than He did! But, I read this to say, there will be more significant numbers of us doing them. Even then, He knew how populated the earth would become and miracles, signs, and wonders, would be multiplied.

How can this be? He gave power, and authority, to all who would believe in His name, to do it, to speak it, and to live it! However, before we can speak it, we have to believe He meant it, and **we have it!** It is entirely up to us; if we are **willing** to **use** it, He will perform it!

I pretty much take it literally, that Jesus meant ME! In the past, whenever I faced a difficult situation, I prayed to the mighty God, somewhere in the sky, hoping He would arrive at my aid just in time. Looking upward while praying, I hoped to catch a glimpse of Him displaying His mighty power, but I never once saw Him racing to help me.

John 14:17 says, once I received the Holy Ghost, God began to live IN me. He said, "...I am with you, but I shall be **in** you." Now, I pray believing He IS in me, and He meant what He said. I then began to pray to the spirit of God that was in me, for it would help me believe and realize, He was truly that close and

He would work through me. It makes it much easier to have faith and believe He hears MY prayers, along with all the other requests going to Heaven's throne. I simply believe, even if it takes a while, He WILL answer! If you have the Holy Ghost, try this. In my mind, I still understand it is God performing the miracles, but He works through me at times, just like He worked through the disciples, who walked and talked with Him on the shores of Galilee. Look what miracles Jesus performed through them in the book of Acts!

We need to get self out of the way! We need to eliminate worry and the taunting questions like, "What if this doesn't work? Everyone is watching!" We need to remind ourselves continually it's not us anyway. If this is going to get done, Jesus will have to do it. This kind of thinking takes the pressure off of us and places it on the One who handles it well. God is the one who receives all the glory!

This past year, Glenn and I have been doing some fellowship in a wonderful community. We simply share with each other what we know about the Word of God and His goodness to each of us. It is a wonderful time of fellowship spent in conversation about things we all seem to enjoy very much.

These precious people are so humble, that many do not speak their prayers out loud at all. In fact, many only read them. Most of them don't realize God desires to use them; in fact, many are not aware the gifts of the Spirit are still in operation today. Of all those we have befriended in this region there is one particular couple that practices prayer for others. Recently, another sweet lady has received the baptism of Holy Ghost and is now learning to pray for her family in this spiritual realm.

13

We are trying to help them realize God intended to use them in this manner.

These are such precious people, and we are also learning much from them. They have such a love for one another. When it comes to helping others, they do not hesitate; they join together and do anything they can. We love spending time talking about the Lord with them. Stepping into their world for a few hours is such a blessing to us. We love it and always leave encouraged and refreshed by their wonderful spirit. Personally, I must admit we do have a few favorites, in this community. Two of these wonderful friends are Samuel and Rachael Smoker. We love them dearly and sometimes we even go out to dinner together. It is a blessing to be with great children of God, who reside in this area. Another precious couple, whom I will simply call, Katie and her husband, are the kindest young couple, we have ever met. The more we have come to know them, the more we love them.

My point is, even though none of us are perfect, God desires to use all of us. He has given many of us spiritual gifts. The enemy of our soul tries continually to take these gifts from our minds. He works in deceptive ways, to either distract us, or hinder us from developing a deeper relationship with God.

I think this is so we won't have time to think about it. The enemy of our soul places worldly things in front of us to entice us, and to prevent us from spending time with Jesus. He knows it will keep us from reaching our full spiritual potential. OH! Did you think YOU, were the only one he tries to trick? Not so. Discouragement is his job, and he does it very well... unless we catch on to him.

As I was praying about this quite a while back, I asked God, "Just how much authority do I actually have?" He said nothing at that moment; but that night, He gave me a dream. I don't believe He gave me this dream to scare me, but to enlighten my mind. I don't feel led to disclose to you the full content of the dream at this time, but God did show me exactly how much power we have as His children.

The dream seemed so real, when I awoke I was very shaken! Then I heard God say , "That much!" With the revelation of knowledge I received at that moment, I knew God had given me a confirmation in my heart. In any situation I faced, in the exact minute I needed it, He would give me the ability to overcome! Keep in mind, this does not mean I should go around unwisely spouting off, "I have power!" God forbid! I genuinely don't think it works that way. However, in a life and death situation, if I called on Him, He would surely stand by me. In fact, He has! Trust me, in my lifetime I should have died many times, BUT GOD watched out for me. Many,who knew full well of my situation, prayed for me and my children every day.

It was such a comfort to me to know people were praying protection over us. I, too, asked God to watch over us. I always knew in my heart, whenever someone who wanted to kill me or intended evil toward me was in the area, for God would warn me. During those times I laid low, knowing it was God trying to protect my children and me.

Once I remarried, my husband, Glenn, purposed to pray for our family every day. Up to this point, he worked the four to twelve shift; therefore, he was always available to pray for the children before they went to school.

Later in my life, I found out many times this person was parked nearby, sitting in a state of rage, just waiting for me to come out the door. It was a miracle; I knew the familiar warning I sensed was God given. When his violent state of mind passed, I would feel it in my spirit and we could go out once again. Jesus, NEVER, failed to warn me. I still thank Him for His protection, and the prayers of my church family, and friends.

This same power ,I felt during the times I called on the Lord for protection, was just as dominant as the outward words of faith I spoke in any adverse circumstances. He was always there when I needed Him.

Now, what about other types of threatening situations like predictions of heavy snow or storms that may produce damaging winds and hail. I certainly don't make a spectacle of myself, so as not to "Let my good be evil spoken of." (Romans 14:16). But I am bold enough to step out on my front porch, and openly rebuke the forecast of hail, destructive winds, or severe lightning. Truthfully, if it is just a little snow, I don't say a word, "snicker, snicker." Storm damage can be very crippling; homes may be lost or flood damage occur...even lives can be lost. It is good to know saints of God can bind together in prayer, and rebuke their severity. I have lost count of storms that have merely died down in seconds! When it happens, it never ceases to amaze me.

Is this the principality of the air, and the powers of darkness God said we have authority over? Yes, it is! Do I continually dwell on these matters? No, however, when winds blow up, whether spiritually or physically, I know who to call on at that moment.

16

*Do I use this knowledge every day? **NO**!!! Just like everyone else, once in a while I FORGET who I am. Suddenly, the Lord reminds me I belong to Him and reassures me of the God given authority He has placed within me. Knowing who is going to back my spoken words of faith, takes away all my fear. I have seen the miraculous happen over and over again. What an honor we have been given, to be able to speak things into existence, or out of it. It is one thing for us just to have this authority, and it is another thing to **believe** we have it, and prayerfully **use** it.*

*You can read all through the Bible, where Jesus taught the disciples to speak the word of faith aloud. Matthew 7:7 says, "Ask, and it shall be given to you..." God gave us the example in Genesis ,when all He used was the power of spoken words to create the earth and everything in it. Think about that; my goodness! God can do so much more than we can think, or imagine. Ephesians 3:20 tells us, "Now unto him, that is able, to do exceeding abundantly above all that we ask, or think according to the power that worketh in **us**." So, is He also telling us even our thoughts are powerful? I believe He is. I think you will agree, allowing ourselves to dwell on negative things, makes us upset and fearful inside. It allows depression to set in our minds. However, if we dream of the great things to come, it enables our hearts, spirits, and minds, to believe our answer will indeed come to pass.*

How many times have we thought of something beautiful, and kept it to ourselves.... for one of two reasons? First, if we spoke it out loud, we feared no one would believe it with us. Secondly, we were afraid someone would call us foolish and destroy the excitement of the dream. Only you can answer that. I personally have done that. There you have it. I said it. What were my reasons for doing this? I felt, as long as I kept it to myself, I could keep the dream alive.

Many times I have been told, "You are such a dreamer." It was the way they stated it that made me feel like it was a disease, or maybe something terrible. However, I refused to let it go; and I just became cautious of who I shared my dreams with. I know, without a doubt, what God has spoken to me, and I will never let them go.

On several occasions, I have felt God impress me to pray for someone, and I have witnessed His miraculous results. I have learned long ago to trust Him. I no longer hesitate and I ignore the enemy's taunting voice that says, "Everyone is watching, you will look foolish if this doesn't work!" No, I just do what He has asked me to do. I set my face like a flint and keep moving forward; I refuse to allow the enemy's false accusations to stop me.

Oh, trust me, I have heard the whispers, and seen the doubtful looks on unbelievers faces. I just had to ignore those things and not allow them to stop me. I attend a church where they love and support me. I can't explain how it happens; I simply pray and Jesus gives me strength to believe.

There are times I do not specifically feel an unction to pray for anyone in particular; I see the need, and understand that immediate prayer is required. I have stepped out of my comfort zone, by faith, and many times the Lord has answered.

We have an acquaintance that called me one night. She said she knew I had great faith. We met at a business meeting and I had spoken to her about the books I had written. She listened intently, while I shared some of my experiences, and it must have transferred faith into her spirit. She was asking me to pray for her daughter, who had a severe health issue! I explained to her I had great faith in my Jesus, but not in myself. I was just flesh and blood like everyone else.

She related her dire circumstances to me. The previous week, as she prepared dinner, her daughter began screaming. Running to the bedroom, fear gripped her heart; for her child was horrified that suddenly she could not see, hear, or walk! When her mom heard her, as a registered nurse, she knew there was something seriously wrong with her.

They immediately put her in their S.U.V. and headed for Johns Hopkins Hospital, in Baltimore, Maryland, about two hours away.

After the girls' testing was completed, they explained to the Mother, that her daughter had Chiari Malformation! It was a condition which caused the tonsils of the brain to drop down inside the skull, crowding the spinal column. It can be severe and in some instances must be dealt with very quickly, as in this case. This condition could rapidly become life threatening! They prepared for her surgery the following Friday, only a week and a day away.

On Thursday, after she had returned from the hospital, she called and asked if I would please pray for her daughter before she went back for more testing on the following Thursday. They needed to do one more MRI to see if the tonsils had dropped down farther and they would be aware of any changes before they went into surgery on Friday.

*The fact she had called for prayer at all,
impressed me to know she had faith in God!*

*Learning I was familiar with Chiari Malformation
astounded her. My precious niece had just been through
this terrible surgery a few years prior. I will admit,
when I heard that was her problem, my heart sank. I
knew from my own family, it was a dire situation. I
learned from my sister, JoAnn, that the tonsils have to
be put back in place very **slowly**, so as not to damage
them any more than they already were. They would
actually have to make room in the skull to accomplish
this procedure. I knew all too well, this surgery was not
a headache we were going to pray about here. If this
miracle was going to happen, we had to give it all to
Jesus. He was the only one who could perform such a
thing!*

*This particular condition in her brain was horrific
to deal with at any time. My sister told me the only way
to correct this was with surgery. The Neurologist, at the
University of Penn in Philadelphia, told them that the
tonsils of the brain would never pull back up on their
own.*

*As I was listening to this Mother's horror story,
my mind was racing in every direction. Sometimes I
think it's better NOT to know too many facts; it gives
you more reason to doubt. However, knowing the
severity of the girl's illness, I had already crossed that
line. I knew the implications, which is why I felt so
panicked.*

*I heard that little voice screaming at me from
within, "Tell her NO! There is no way you and
Glenn, can pray for this girl."*

Now, while I appeared entirely confident to her on

the phone, inside I was in full panic mode! How could we
ever pray such a prayer, expecting it to work? We knew
very well the physician said it never pulled back up on
its own. Plus, knowing all the complications that could
occur during the surgery was terrifying!

Then, it hit me. WE didn't have to heal this girl;
we only had to pray to the "ONE", I knew could do this!
Here I was panicking for nothing! It was never up to me,
or Glenn. All we had to do was ask HIM, in faith
believing. Suddenly, all the negative thoughts in my
mind to tell her "NO" left. The urgency to deny the
Mothers request, was replaced with a quiet sense of
peace and trust.

To be perfectly honest with you, I was so glad we
were not responsible to heal this young lady; we
simply had to believe nothing was impossible to God,
and He would perform the miracle. It was entirely up to
Him and Him alone.

Keeping this totally in my mind, relieved my own
pressure. We only had to hand it to Him, and this is the
one thing we could certainly do. The rest of that week,
we prayed earnestly for the pending Monday evening,
she was coming for prayer. In this particular situation,
we felt as though we were in the will of God. However,
we do not question the Lord, if our prayer does not
always have an immediate result. Sometimes, He has a
different plan.

When she knocked on my door, we greeted her
with a smile of confidence. I must say this girl was
beautiful... just beautiful! It was hard to comprehend
this twenty- one year old girl, with her entire life ahead
of her, was so ill. I told her we would be happy to pray
for her, so long as she understood; if she received her

healing it was Jesus, who performed it. I also explained to her, if He didn't heal her at that moment, it was His call. We would not question it, and if that is what He chose to do, she could not be angry with us. Again, she agreed.

Looking at her in this vulnerable moment, my heart was overwhelmed with compassion. I thought to myself, "I can't think of one reason He would not heal this precious girl."

We asked her to please be seated on a very large rolling hassock I had in my living room. Along with her hopeful Mother, and our mutual friend Capriecia, Glenn, and I laid hands on this girl and prayed the prayer of faith and healing, in our own way. NOW, keep in mind, as I have previously stated, the Bible says "...Do not pray amiss!..." (James 4:3) Merely saying, "OH, God, touch her," is praying amiss.

We prayed explicitly for him to **slowly and gently pull these tonsils** *back up out of the spinal cord, and into her brain, so as not to cause any more damage. "Lord, please heal her this night so she won't have to endure such a traumatic surgery." We asked it in the name of Jesus Christ, praising Him as if He had already done it, and said, "Amen."*

We felt nothing; she saw no evidence that she was healed, but Thursdays MRI would tell the story!

They went in for the testing and anxiously awaited for the doctor to disclose new results. The neurologist came out and related to them, "We are not exactly sure what is going on here. The tonsils have started to pull **slowly,** *back up into the brain." There's that word* **slowly.** *He continued saying, "This is very unusual. In fact, this has never happened! However,*

since it has, this is no longer a life or death situation."
Because this was the week before Thanksgiving, he said,
"I think we should let her enjoy the holidays, and we will
recheck it the first week in January. If you have any
problems in the meantime, please contact us right
away."
    Now, as a Mother, I don't even have to tell you
how happy they were. The Mother called me that night
and was beside herself, with joy!
    The holidays passed, and they returned for their
new examination. They did another MRI that revealed
the tonsils had pulled almost entirely back up into the
brain! The doctor told them, "This has never happened!
You don't understand," he said, "It has never happened
here or anywhere in the world!   This does NOT happen!
The only way the brain can be repaired is for us to put
the tonsils back in place by surgery!" The Mother spoke
up, "She was prayed for." He looked at her and said,
"That is the only way it could have happened." I can't
tell you how happy that Mama was. I was overcome with
joy myself, as we gave Jesus the glory. I continue to
thank Him to this day! What a miracle!
    God has given each of us authority to use the
power of the spoken word. It is indeed a gift within us,
but it's up to us if we choose to exercise it or not. If we
will pray and believe, we will grow spiritually. It will
allow the Lord to take us to wonderful places in the
Spirit, we never dreamed possible.
    Let us not make the mistake of setting the
God given, authority aside, allowing it to set dormant on
the shelf of our hearts and never use it. There is so much
power walking around in the world that is entirely
wasted, only because we are fooled by the enemy of our

soul into believing, when God gave out spiritual authority, we dare to even think He meant "US". We need to quit categorizing it in our minds. For example, "Well, that man needs his hip prayed for, I can do that. But that man is blind! I'm not going to touch that one, no sir! The baby has a fever, let's pray. However, that four year old child needs her spine straightened. Umm, I'll leave that to someone else." A miracle is just that...a miracle! Jesus doesn't need us to line up the easy ones. He can do the impossible for anyone who believes!

I attended a deaf ministry conference this past week. I saw hundreds of deaf people. I thought to myself, how many of these people came, hoping for a miracle? How many will be brave enough to ask for prayer? How many will go home having been touched by God, of course, but how many will be healed?

As I sat there, I wondered, who would be brave enough to offer to pray for them, including myself. Then I began to think about moving around and praying for some of these precious saints of God.

*Now please understand, I am NOT being critical! I am very serious. I am using myself to research how I felt, and why it was so hard for **me** to pray for any of them. Here is what I discovered. I made up my mind: I was going to at least try. I have no idea how many felt the same way I did, but I am sure there were many.*

At the altar call, as I made my way towards the front, I felt such a barrage of questions attacking my mind. Like, "Who do you think you are?" As I passed one woman praying in the aisle, I wanted to reach for her, but the thought hit my mind, she will be so very disappointed if you pray for her and she doesn't receive her healing. I fought to override that negative feeling and gently touched her ear that was closest to me, and I prayed. As I moved away from her, the enemy's accusations continued in my mind, "What can you be thinking? You cannot do this!" I continued down the aisle towards the altar. I fought these terrible distractions, and I found three more people to pray for. Did any of them receive their healing? I don't even know! But it wasn't because I didn't step out in faith and at least try. Jesus may touch them in their sleep tomorrow, for all I know. But it let me experience what each person, who steps out to pray for someone, goes through when their hearts want to pray, but their minds keep them in their seats.

As humans, we can have so much faith one week, and the next week we are completely void of our hope, and trust. How can this happen to us? Well, this is just a theory of my own, but I think it hits pretty close to home. When we pray, it makes us feel good inside to know that we communicated with God, as we should. Then... we mess up. Sometimes it is a little; sometimes it is a lot! Now we are thinking, "Oh, how can I be used now, I have royally messed up!" Now, we already know God saw it all; but we are ashamed to go before Him in prayer. This is all the enemy of our soul needs! He is on us; like a shadow, he makes sure we can't feel him breathing down our neck. But he is there!

Now.... his job really kicks in. He begins to accuse the brethren. He blows our mistake way out of proportion in our minds. Then, he reminds us of everything we have ever done wrong. He keeps us from a peaceful sleep. Depending on our personality, he takes our appetite away or causes us to eat more. He lays such a guilt trip on us, we may never find our way back; so we might as well give up. We begin to think, "I am never going to do anything right!" I have to ask you this. Am I the only one He has ever tricked in the past? I don't think so.

Finally, after way too long a wait, at rock bottom, we kick him out again and find our way back to the foot of the cross. But we let it drop right there. Next time, you need to give him a rocking that he will never forget. Pull out that God given authority and rock hell, in the name of Jesus! Make him tremble, just to know you are awake.

I have a motto; if you get out of bed with your spiritual fist drawn, the first punch is yours! I heard something like this said in a movie we borrowed one time. I liked it, and improvised it! Still, we forget at times who we are. We can't stay in that place. We must pull ourselves out of a negative realm.

How many people will suffer if you don't get back up? How many children will follow your footsteps? Will there be anyone who will help the Pastor preach this week because they are all bound? The last time I checked, we were all meant to win! Let us pray till hell quivers, and know, that yours was one of the prayers that rocked it! Your prayers are valuable. The kingdom of God depends on them. Your Pastor depends on them. People, who may be weary, rely on your prayers for strength. Make up your mind; if you are the last one standing, your prayers will still make a difference.

This week, instead of going to church hoping God will give you what you need, take your sword with you, and walk in the fullness of His spirit. With God's help, fight and win the spiritual battle! YOU be the one to make the difference this week.

*Someone there will live, because of the God given power **you used**. YOU, throw a spiritual lifesaver to a drowning soul and help them to make it. It will give you such strength, within your soul. You will both be lifted up.*

This power of the spoken word, this wasted, unused authority, will move any spiritual mountain you have before you, if you simply use it, as God desires.

Remember who your Spiritual Daddy is, then set that crown upright, and move forward in Jesus Name.

You, have the honor and are in charge of pushing back all unrighteousness. Your authority will help you pray for the sick, watch Jesus move on them, and witness them recover.

Don't spend one more day wasting the power and authority God has given you. Use it to change your world. Allow Jesus to make this world a better place, just because you lived in it. Do it all in Jesus name; He is undoubtedly with you!

The Gift Only God Could Have Given Her

~~~~~~

I have a bittersweet story to tell. If we will listen for that soft calling voice, God can use us in many ways, any time He chooses. You must learn to train the ear of your heart to know His sweet voice. You will be amazed how many times a day He will speak to you. Even though you may not always be aware it is Him, He directs our paths daily. This story tells about one time, when God spoke something to me that was completely unexpected. If indeed, it was Him, I had to choose to obey or miss this opportunity forever.

If it only affected Glenn or me, it would be sad enough. But, when God speaks to us out of the normal to do something that will affect others, somehow we allow our human side to say, "I'm not sure this was you God." In your heart, you now realize if you don't respond, someone else might miss a tremendous blessing, only because you refused to fulfill what He asked you to do. It doesn't leave a very good feeling within.

This generated vicious cycle of self-condemnation and a burden began to grow in my spirit. Why? Because I realized there may never be another opportunity to do what He asked of me. So then, not only did the intended heart miss their blessing, but I lost mine also, for not obeying.

Jesus has spoken to me many times before, and I knew without a doubt it was Him, but this particular time, I wasn't quite sure. I could have felt this way because to accept what He whispered to me hurt my heart deeply. I did not want to listen to this!

28

Maybe I could deal with it another time, but not today. Still, as He continued to speak, I could not deny it was Him!

I have a very dear friend I met about three years earlier at the Century Club meeting. I will call her Precious, because that is what she is.

Precious had a sick husband that continued a downward spiral in his health. He would soon need the kind of help, which was more than she could give. She had to make arrangements to place him in a nursing home. She confided to me, he had begun to wander, especially at night, and she was afraid to fall asleep, for fear she would not hear him go out the door. Realizing his confinement to the nursing home was approaching soon, they purchased a home nearby the facility. After his change of residence, Precious visited him every day except Thursdays, which was her errand day. Being elderly herself, she was too exhausted to visit with him afterward.

Each day she was there, she patiently fed him. Sometimes it would take over an hour to get nourishment in him. Still, that never stopped her from trying. She was always determined, he would eat and most times he finally did.

Well, this particular day, I was standing at my sink, and the only thoughts consuming my mind were how pretty the flowers were, Glenn had just bought me for Valentine's Day. He had never chosen this color for me before. I usually received long stem pink or red roses, but these were between a beautiful peach and pale orange color. They were gorgeous!

At this moment, the Lord spoke to me. I was to take a few of those pretty flowers and put them in a vase

for Precious! He revealed to me, her husband would not
be with her this coming Christmas! Knowing how much
she loved him, as the Lord continued to speak, I sucked
my breath in. He whispered, "Their sons will not think
about her being a Valentine. They will only think about
their own wives.

I want you to write her a love letter from her
husband. Write about the things she has told you of
their good times together, take it to him to sign it, and
give it to her today." Well, I thought, "This can't be you,
God," because like I said, I could hardly bear the thought
of her future heartache. After a few moments of dealing
with my indecision, I knew what I had to do. Like it or
not! After pondering a few moments, I knew I wanted to
obey the Lord, but the knowledge of his coming death
overwhelmed my heart.

Because she was there every day most of the
afternoon, until he finished his dinner around five, we
waited for her to go home. We prayed in the car together
that Jesus would help him to comprehend our request. I
knew, if God said to do this, He would bring this man
out of his fog to be **able** to at least understand what we
wanted him to do. It was quite out of the normal for us,
and took considerable faith on our part.

We entered the nursing home through the rear
door, so Precious could not see our car from her
residence. I left the roses in the car and requested to see
her husband. They informed us Precious had just left
and perhaps they could catch her; but we stopped them,
and explained to them what we hoped to do.

Knowing the actual mental state he was in at
the time, their smiles faded, and were quickly replaced
with a look of sadness.

It turned out, he was actually walking right ahead of us in the same hallway. The nurses took him by the hand and led him to a nearby table, where we wanted to sit.

I called him by name, but he was really out of touch at this moment. We sat down at the table together, and I said, "I want to read you a love letter I wrote to Precious from you." At first he had a blank stare; as I began to read the letter, he perked up! I talked in the letter as though I was him writing it. I spoke of how many fun times we had raising our three sons, and the trips we took together. I recalled many stories about her life she had previously shared with me. I went on; "I remember the time we flew in a small plane from Maine to Easton, Maryland, with friends, just to have dinner at our favorite restaurant and then flew back home. Remember all of those beautiful trips to Florida? Do you know how thankful I am our sons turned out to be great adults, and how proud I am of them all?" I then went on to say, "Thank you for the beautiful years we had together." I don't remember exactly all that was written in the letter, as I didn't save it on my computer. It was personal and just for her.

Once I stopped reading it, he looked at me and said, "That is beautiful!" At first, we were shocked! I told him, "Today is Valentine's Day, and this is a love letter. It is from you to Precious." This time when I said it, I saw the light of recognition flicker in his eyes, and knew he understood what it was. I told him I wanted him to sign it for me. I handed him the pen, and he touched the paper where I pointed. He made a tiny little line up and down. He glanced up at me, knowing he had not done it right. I said, "Try again, Honey," but he made another mark the very same way.

The real miracle of this story, is he looked at me and said, "Help me, PLEASE!" He said it with such feeling I knew, that HE knew, exactly what he was doing. I sat there for a second trying to think how I should go about this! I know it was God that spoke the answer to me. "Lay his hand on top of yours while you write his name." So I did just that! He laid his shaky hand on mine, and I signed love and his name. He said, "Thank you." He knew without a doubt what he had just done; then his mind was gone again.

We took the flowers to Precious, and I told her God had put it on my heart to do this; however, I never mentioned to her the rest of what Jesus spoke to me that day. If it was indeed God, we would all deal with that soon enough!

Her reaction was so touching to my heart. I could tell by watching her she was greatly moved; I knew I had done the right thing. I realized at this moment; it was indeed a God thing. As it turned out, those beautiful roses were HER favorite color! I suddenly understood why Glenn had chosen that color, without knowing the reason himself. Jesus had orchestrated this entire happening from the start to the finish! It was very kind of God to let us know he had indeed been in this from the beginning. Jesus verified it to us in such a beautiful way, He had definitely used us to minister to Precious and her husband that day.

This past spring, God picked this flower, and took him on Home to bloom forever more with Him. Just as He had revealed to me, he was not with her at Christmas. He loved the Lord with all of his heart and happily lived for Him the best he knew how.

We still watch out for Precious. She is still going strong. I obeyed the voice of the Lord, and I have never been happier. I know without a doubt, she will forever cherish the beautiful love letter signed by her husband. I believe each time she pulls it out, she will feel his love, over and over again. It will strengthen her, until they are together forever in that city, where the Lamb is the Light.

Sometimes God Chooses the Foolish Things To Confound the Wise

~~~~~~

A couple of years ago, Glenn and I began teaching a Bible study for one of the dearest and sweetest families we have ever met. We were having the Bible study at one of the daughter's homes. As it turned out, nine members of them have been baptized, in Jesus name, and four of them have been filled with the baptism of the Holy Spirit. Several of this large, loving family attends our services. We are thrilled, and we love them all very much.

In the early days of summer, the Father of this great family, Dale, called me on the phone. He was beside himself with panic. At first, because he was so upset, I didn't even recognize his voice. He explained to me that his brother was in the Peninsula Hospital, in Salisbury, Maryland, and the entire left side of his heart had stopped working. They wanted the man's wife, to let them unplug the breathing machine. The family had been told there was NO HOPE!

She called them on their vacation in Florida, and told Dale she just could not do it! He assured her he would have some friends come and pray for her husband. Those friends were Glenn and I, his Bible study teachers.

Now, keep in mind, we were trying to teach them they could call on Jesus for anything. The beautiful thing about this was, they believed us. They entirely trusted we would only teach them Biblical truth. So,

34

now here he was... testing his new found faith. The only problem was, he was in Florida, and we were in Delaware. Of course, I told him we would go that very day, right away.

Now, let me explain our dilemma to you. Get ready for it! Glenn has terrible trouble with his knees, and because he knew I was facing surgery on my hip, he was trying to delay his surgical knee repair. So, at the time, we were a pretty sad looking, pathetic, limping couple.

We could not refuse, because Dale had such confidence in Jesus; but at this moment, considering our circumstances, we felt seriously inadequate within ourselves. Still, we knew we had to at least try. How could we tell him no, when this was the first time he called on us in need of prayer?

From our standpoint, we could hardly walk. How was this going to look? I'll tell you how it was going to look; it was going to look crazy! It was going to look embarrassing! I was already so self-conscious about not being able to walk. While we were getting ready to go, we were talking about how silly this was going to appear to people; two limping people, praying the prayer of faith for the dying, just isn't your norm. We simply could not tell this new trusting babe in the Lord, "NO!"

In II Timothy 4:2, the Bible says to "...be instant in season, and out of season..." Well, this was about as "out", as we have ever been. I was already fighting my embarrassment, and we hadn't even left the house. That feeling continued to nag us all the way there. The hospital was about an hour away; Glenn drove, and I prayed. We made a deal with each other; when we arrived, we would not ask to speak to the family members. Since they did not know us, and we would not recognize them, we could be in and out of the hospital room with no negative (and rightfully justified) looks. I mean after all, how was it going to appear to the family and nursing staff? Two seriously limping people, who needed healing themselves, were there requesting to pray for someone else's healing? Trust me, if anyone knew how ridiculous that would seem, we did! We finally reached the hospital.

Once we were parked and hobbled our way into the hospital, we were informed the Cardiology department we were to visit, was clear over on the other side of the building. That was on the other side of the city block! I had just spent every ounce of personal pain tolerance I had, to get from the car to the building. UGH! There was no way I could walk at least one half a mile to the Cardiology unit.

So "MR. G." (my pet name for him) decided he would use a **wheelchair** and **push** me. We were now in the hospital lobby, so I couldn't make a scene about it; my goodness, we were there to PRAY! I know it sounds funny right now, but I assure you it was NOT funny at that moment. The only thing worse to me than walking with my obvious limp; was riding in a wheelchair and suffering from the curious stares of total strangers. I was so embarrassed! I would have rather died than to have to ride in that chair.

When it comes to things like this, I have always been too proud to ask for help. I was usually determined to keep on moving. But now it reached a point, it was no longer a choice. We had two options. One, was to turn around and go home and admit to our new babe in the Lord we never prayed for the man. Or two, to swallow

*our pride (more mine than his) and do what had been
asked of us to do. There was no choice; we had to do this.
Our confidence was far greater in Jesus, than anything
we could do. Even when we are between a rock and a
hard place, there is no time or situation that is a
problem for Jesus! The Lord is always in season. We
chose to go ahead and pray, as WE were not the ones,
who were going to heal the man, anyway! If he was to
live, it would definitely be only a touch from Jesus, that
would bring him out of this critical situation.*

*We went through the halls, and finally arrived at
the Heart Unit waiting room. We made our way toward
the patient rooms. We knew his family was watching us
go through the waiting room; but as we had agreed
earlier we said nothing. Once we were past the family
and in the heart unit, I saw a nurse's aide and asked her
which room was Mr. Gladden's. She pointed to the
curtain right in front of us, and told us she had just
finished attending to him. I said to her, "We are here to
pray for this man." She looked at us pitifully, because
she knew he was dying. She whispered, "He is in a coma,
you know." We nodded in acknowledgment, and entered
the cubicle. Closing the curtain behind us, we left the
wheelchair outside the tiny unit.*

*This poor man looked awful! He did not have a
clear place on his arms to enable us to even touch him!
We were fearful of hurting his skin or bruising him
more. There was blood under the skin surface, and it
was actually more red than bruised. I looked at him and
decided to touch the top of his head gently; I spoke his
name quietly.*

*Now, here is where Jesus completely took
over! Surprisingly, the patient opened his eyes. I spoke*

to him softly, and informed him that his brother, Dale, had asked us to come and pray for him. He gave us the slightest nod of his head. I asked, "Is it okay if we pray for you?" Again, he slightly nodded his head and closed his eyes. So, the two "Nothings," that had limped their way to this poor man, put their hands on the top of his head and began to call on Jesus to reach down and touch him. We do not like to pray amiss! I asked the Lord, "Please touch the left side of his heart, and make it beat PERFECTLY. Bring him out of this horrible condition he is in, and give him hope. Dear Jesus, please heal him and let him recognize his family again, so that his brother, Dale, will know the power of God is real!"

There were no fireworks, no sign from God... no, not even so much as a cold chill signaling His presence; we felt nothing. Still, we had an inner confidence in Jesus, as we had been in situations like this before. We did as Dale had asked, and it was all up to Jesus now.

Glenn settled me back in that wretched wheelchair, and we headed out of the unit for a return slap of humiliation, and embarrassment. Pushing me, Glenn simply limped back out through the waiting room, past his family, who was still sitting there. We stuck to our decision not to introduce ourselves, for fear just the glances we would rightfully get, would hinder our own faith. We made it back to the car; Glenn drove, while I prayed and thanked Jesus for this miracle most of the way home.

For the next two or three days, we waited for news about this man. It came on Saturday, while we were having a yard sale; Dale called me. When I heard his voice, I automatically sucked in my breath. He conveyed to me his brother was sitting up in a chair! He was breathing on his own, and unhooked from all his equipment, entirely awake and eating real food!

Dale related to me, as soon as he heard his brother was out of the coma and doing better, he made a request to his nephew. He wanted him to ask his doctor to repeat the test that verified the left side of his heart was dead, and it would never come back. This doctor was the same physician, who had advised them that they needed to unplug him from the machine. Dale didn't call me until the test results came in.

In fact, the doctor had just left the man's room, and had stated, "The new test results are in and the left side of the heart has come back and is beating perfectly. It is truly a miracle." Just like we had prayed...the physician even used the word "perfectly"!

This man told the Cardiologist, in front of the charge nurse that day, "I remember a man and a woman came into my room and prayed for me. They touched the top of my head, and I woke up when they prayed." The nurse chimed in, "No! No one came in to pray for you; I was at the desk the entire time." But of course, he was right. When we arrived, there was no nurse at the desk, there was only the attendant, just outside his room. This is why we asked the aide which room he was in. We were not in there even five minutes; we left very quickly so that he could rest. We prayed, and then we were gone.

This healing was indeed a miracle from the hand of God that day. The man had been bed bound for months, and was very weak. His muscles were atrophied, and he passed away a few months later.

While we were sad to hear this, he told his brother, Dale, had he died "that" day, he would not have been ready to meet God, and that the Lord was so kind to bring him back from the point of death. He made his heart right with the Lord; this news meant the world to Dale, and to his brother's children.

The only thing good about us that day, was no matter how we felt or appeared to others, we obeyed, the voice of the Lord. God showed us clearly, that as I Corinthians 1:27 says, "But God hath chosen the foolish things of the world to confound the wise..."

Dear Jesus, let us always be foolish, if that is the way you choose to use us. While in ourselves, we are very inadequate...we are completely confident in the "ONE", who goes before us!

It is hard to believe, with all of our flaws, He is willing to use us, but I guess the day we feel we ARE adequate enough, is the day we need go back to the foot of the cross, and humble ourselves again before the Master.

What is it that you need? Just ask, genuinely believing He heard your petition, and if it is His will, He will answer. He has not responded to every prayer we have ever prayed. God has a time and a reason for everything. We have many "prayers in waiting". However, He has honored many requests for us! We will always at least try.

A Lesson About Praise and,
Its Effects On God

~~~~~~

This is a story about prayer and praise, and how it affects God. I have often heard it preached from many pulpits, how important our praises are to God.

I have wondered many times in my life, how MY praise could do anything for God. After all, He is the Creator of the universe. I found it hard to believe that anything I can do, can truly help God. I know in myself, I can't do anything good without HIM! Yet, I hear how we need to praise Him and bless Him. This thought has always intrigued me.

One day in prayer, I decided to ask Jesus, "What can my praise do to help you? It is just me, Patty. As a human being, with so many limitations, I feel very inadequate to be able to bless YOU. Yet, I read in your word, **Psalms 103:1 "Bless the Lord, O my soul, with all that is within me, bless your Holy name.** *" It is hard for me to comprehend that simply speaking these words, from a regular human beings point of view, can actually bless YOU! How can this be, Lord? There is nothing you can't do. There is absolutely nothing I can think of that you could possibly need, you can't speak into existence for yourself. So how can I bless you? I can speak the words of love and adoration I feel for You toward Heaven; but how do these things bless You, who needs nothing or no one?" As I pondered this thought, He began to speak to me gently.*

"Remember the vision you had about Brother Greg? (Book two, "No More Crumbs") Remember the

*power that you saw coming from his mouth? The very
same power that you saw shooting from his lips, when
he rebuked the enemy, is the very same power that
comes from you when you praise and worship Me! Your
lips send that power (virtue) back to me."*

*As I thought about this incident with Brother
Greg, I remembered at the end of a Sunday school class,
he started to rebuke the enemy of his soul outwardly. I
remember seeing lightning bolts, and mighty rushing
waters shooting from his mouth! It was moving so
swiftly, with such mighty power, that it flowed to the
back of the church and never once touched the floor!   It
was so shocking; I could hardly believe my eyes! I knew
it was a vision from the Lord.*

*Now, God was telling me the very same power
that came from Brother Greg's mouth, to fight spiritual
wickedness, was the same kind of power that came from
our mouths, when we direct it as praise to Him! To me,
this was the most exciting lesson I had ever learned from
God.*

*It makes me feel great inside to know, when the
spirits of darkness attack our minds, He wants us to feel
powerful...not helpless!*

*The words that we speak are very powerful,
whether we realize it or not. We need to be very careful
of what we speak. Do not utter curses on your own
children, or anyone else. When Jesus said, Proverbs:
12:14 "A man shall be satisfied with good by the fruit of
his mouth:....," He meant it! Fruit in this Scripture isn't
what we eat, but what we speak! Please, choose your
words wisely.*

*Think before you utter anything negative to
anyone. I still have not entirely overcome this myself,*

but I am seriously working on it. Speak positive, because the words you speak have the power to become fulfilled.

When you are speaking to the enemy of your soul, don't be afraid to lay it on him! This can ONLY be done by pleading the blood of Jesus; we have the power...but not within OUR flesh. Let your prayers be so compelling the enemy shudders the moment he realizes you're awake. We have permission to rock Hell with our spoken words. I have a little saying you will see a couple of times in this book, so you will remember it. <u>When dealing with the enemy of your soul ,if you get out of bed in the morning with your spiritual fist drawn, the first punch is yours! Don't be afraid to use it, and use it well! The only way to do this, is to start your day in prayer!</u>

You will find it brings you great pleasure to know, as a child of God, you are the stronger one. Always be sure to thank Jesus for this honor.

I am going to break down some Scripture verses here, so pay very close attention, as it will enlighten the rest of your life. I heard a visiting minister from Rockville, Maryland speak this wonderful lesson, that will stay with me forever.

Psalms 149;1-9

1. Praise *ye the Lord. Sing unto the Lord a new song, and his praise in the congregation of saints.*

2. *Let Israel rejoice in him that made him: let the children of Zion be joyful in their King.*

3. *Let them praise his name in the dance: let them sing praises unto him with the trimbrel and harp.*

4.*For the Lord taketh pleasure in his people: He will beautify the meek with salvation.*

5.*Let the Saints be joyful in glory: let them sing aloud upon their beds.*

6.Let the high praises of God be in their mouth, and a two-edged sword in their hand

We will pause here for just a moment. In these first six verses, God has told us **what** we should do. The next three verses He explains to us the **why** we need to do this. When broken down like this, it makes it a very powerful tool to fight the enemy.

7. (WHY)..To execute vengeance upon the heathen, and punishments upon the people;
8. To bind their kings with chains, and their nobles with fetters of iron:
9. To execute upon them the judgment written: this honor have all his saints. Praise ye the Lord."

What the Psalmist is saying here, is when "something", such as depression, carnality, oppression, or perhaps an individual, comes in to disrupt a service, or mock God, our praise actually binds that spirit. Whatever method he chooses, our praise keeps him from hindering a great move of God in our services. It doesn't say it runs spiritual darkness out of there; it says He binds them with spiritual chains, and fetters of iron.

Does this mean they have to sit there and let all the praise, worship, and the word of God flow through their ugly ears? I like to think so anyway. Praise, genuine praise, is what brings the glory of God into the sanctuary. At the end of Psalms 149:9 The Lord went so far as to say, "This honor has all of his saints."

My pastor, Rev. Royce Andrus, says if we bind the enemy, he will get tired of listening to our praise and quit coming to hinder! If you have never heard it explained this way, I pray it will bless your soul, and encourage you to praise God in a new way.

Do your part to help the great word of God go forth in

every service, by using your voice in outward praise and worship.

I have found that people become very loud and excited at a football game or concert. Why, even at an amusement park we squeal with pure delight on a thrilling ride! There are many things the human flesh cheers on. We are not embarrassed to openly cheer things that excite us. There is nothing at all wrong with this. God wants us to be happy and have fun together. It strengthens us. I have heard it said, that laughter is good for the marrow of the bones!

However, this particular Psalm tells us the many ways we are to praise him; none of which are silent. I'm not sure where the phase, "silent praise", entered the sanctuary. It's not in my Bible, or yours either. I only know that all of our Bibles encourage us over and over again to outwardly praise the Lord. I firmly believe it is important; He included it in the Bible for a reason.

I pray that this will enlighten your heart and you realize God has a purpose for everything. In ourselves, who would have ever thought our praise could stop the devil dead in his tracks? I like to dwell on that thought.

I have seen many miracles in our sanctuary. I have been present in several services and watched, as singing and outward praise ushered in the presence of God. This kind of worship should be prevalent in every church. Trust me, I have visited some pretty dead churches, and listened to dried up sermons. If you are honest with yourself, you have, too.

One church I visited wasn't dead, as far as laughter was concerned. If the impact depended on laughter, the church was fully alive! However, the preacher popped one joke after another for the entire service! I left, realizing I had laughed the whole service; but not once did I feel the presence of God, which was the reason I went to church in the first place.

Everyone left there so happy because they had spent the morning laughing; endorphins were freely flowing. But, by the time they reached their door, they most likely couldn't even recall what the sermon was about. People in great need returned home in the same spiritual condition they came. Why? First, because there was no sincere prayer and worship to invite Him into their presence. God was not the focal point; drawing nearer TO Him was not as important, as what He could do FOR them.

I encourage you to search the Scriptures for yourself. Even in your own personal prayer time, entering into His gates with outward praise and worship are crucial factors in attracting the presence of the Lord. There are many examples in the Word of God. Try Him, and see if it doesn't make a significant difference in every service.

That's why David said, Psalms 122:1 "I was glad when they said unto me, Let us go into the house of the Lord." There is a lot of meaning in this verse. It is wonderful to think we are going to get a spiritual lift; we all need them. But it takes on a whole new meaning to believe our praise sends power back to God, and lifting Him up releases His hands to answer our prayers.

I will take it one step farther; I praise Him the same way right in my home. That is where I spend most of my time in prayer. After all He has done for me, why wouldn't I want to send power and virtue back to Him?

It says in His Word, that if we don't praise Him, He will cause the rocks to cry out. There is No rock going to take my place in praise.

I shall always try to do what He asks of me and more. I am happy and honored to praise His Holy Name. I want my prayers to be uninhibited, and freely given...not just to receive a blessing... but to BE a blessing to Him. He asks so little of me; it is the very least I can do for his kingdom. His written word says in, Romans 12;1 "...It is our reasonable service." My husband and I have tried to instill the concept of this Scripture in our children. Even though He loves to give, praise is not just about getting something from God...it is more about giving something to Him. All he wants is YOU!

It Was Nice to Be Someone Else's Blessing

~~~~~~

When you live life every day, depending on God for everything, the surprises and miracles He sends your way never cease to amaze you.

Many times in our lives, we have depended entirely on answered prayers from God. We asked the Lord for something we needed, and we thanked Him in faith believing He would answer. When He supplies it in ways that we would never expect, it always seems almost surreal. Once you have experienced miraculous answers, and your mind begins to digest God truly orchestrated it from the beginning, it is so amazing!

When we yield ourselves to Him, I am so thankful he is able to use us. I especially love the days He orders our steps, so we can become His hands and feet. We walk in total faith, believing the moment He needs us...we will know! The amazing part of this story was, on this particular day, He ordered our steps to become someone else's blessing.

My husband, Glenn, and I had gone to the local grocery store to do our mid-week shopping. You know, to pick up those few things you need, that you forgot to place on your list the last time you were there.

As we made our way through the store, we kept passing the same young couple in each aisle going the opposite direction. This happens often in a grocery store. Normally, I will say, "Now look, we have to quit meeting like this." We usually both chuckle and move on. This particular couple had a very small newborn in a car seat, perched on top of the cart. I felt very drawn to them. After I commented how cute their baby was, they thanked me and moved on. I assumed I was merely relating to them because we had two babies at home. Our twins were only one year old, and their big sister and brother were taking care of them for the short time we were to be gone. If you have had a baby, you will certainly understand what a treat it was, simply to get out... even for a few minutes, without a child in tow. We had two infants, and a trip to the grocery store or taking a walk to the mailbox was always a nice change of scenery. I think you know exactly what I'm talking about here.

As we approached the check out, we noticed the same young couple, with the adorable infant, was in line directly in front of us. As they got to the register to pay for their groceries, I could not help but notice all they were buying was one pack of hot dogs, one loaf of bread, and two cans of infant formula.

The young man reached into his pocket to get the money to pay for his purchase; I watched him sheepishly count it and then put one can of formula back.

It was at this moment, I realized their purchase of bread and hotdogs was to be their supper for the next few nights. Today was Wednesday, and I surmised, most likely, he would not receive a paycheck until Friday. I realized this young man had just made a painful decision. Having twin babies myself, and knowing the cost of formula, I knew these kids needed help feeding their precious baby.

It was at this moment I also realized, the unused formula I had in my cupboard, was the same exact brand he had just removed from the conveyer belt and placed *on a nearby shelf, before it reached the cashier. My twins had been switched to whole milk and we had several cans of formula left, because I didn't know anyone to give it to. Since I didn't have the receipt anymore, I couldn't return it. I kept it on hand, just in case anyone we knew might need it sometime in the future. In my heart, I knew we would eventually find someone who could use it. It was so expensive; we were certainly NOT going to throw it away. We hoped it would be a blessing to someone down the road.*

It was at this point, that it all came together in my mind and I realized God, in his great wisdom, had placed us in a position to be a miracle for someone else.

Being the Mother and brave soul that I am, I tapped the young man on the shoulder. I was trying very hard to word this correctly, so I would not offend or humiliate him. I said, "Excuse me, Sir. I couldn't help but notice the brand of formula you use to feed your baby. At birth, my twins were placed on that, too. About a month ago, the pediatrician switched them to whole milk, and I have about twenty cans of that same formula at home. The date has not expired and if you could use it, I would truly love to give it to you."

Let me tell you, that young man lit up like a light bulb! He answered me, "Are you for real, Lady?" I responded, "I most certainly am!" He quickly took the other can of formula they were going to purchase, and placed it on the shelf beside the first one. He said, "Yes, Ma'am, we could sure use it!" I explained to him, we lived up the road, right on the main highway, and if he didn't mind following us home, Glenn would bring it out to him. After all, I didn't want them to think they would have to enter a stranger's house. It's sad, but this is the world we now live in.

Having walked in the shoes of need often enough ourselves, this was one time; we could be a blessing to others. We felt so good in our hearts to be in a position to help this young couple. I think we were as happy as they were. In fact, I am sure of it.

They followed us to our home and Glenn retrieved the box of formula from the bottom of the kitchen cupboard. When Glenn handed it to that young man, the look I saw on their faces displayed their very grateful hearts.

As he accepted the box from Glenn's hands, he said, "Lady, you have no idea what you have just done!" I replied, "Oh, I think maybe I do!" I simply smiled, as they put it in their car.

In my heart, I knew that God had just allowed us to provide about a month's worth of food for that newborn baby girl. They thanked us and told us they were Christians. They belonged to a church many of my own cousins attended, and had been praying for God to help them. This experience let me know just how orchestrated God's ways truly are.

As they backed out of the driveway, we could still see the smile on their faces. Being a Mother, myself, I knew even those hotdogs were going to taste extra special! I also knew, because there was enough formula in the house to feed their baby for a month, they were going to sleep much better that night. I am sure it also taught them, that Jesus heard them, and answered their heartfelt prayers.

Until the moment I tapped on his shoulder, after the can of formula they were buying was gone, they had no idea what they would feed their baby. For a child that young, it may have lasted a day and a half. But, JESUS saw it all and, without that precious couple knowing it, He ordered their steps that day! They were totally unaware of the blessing that was coming. They simply walked those ordered steps, and together a miracle happened.

The Lord ordered our steps "that day", too! I love it when God shows up!. While after thirty-three years, I no longer remember their names, as I write this, I can still see the smile on their faces. It still warms my heart to know how God brought it all together that day.

If you will pray for Him to use you, He can orchestrate a miracle. Ask Him to order your steps and, when the need arises, God will allow you to be a blessing to someone, too. I wouldn't trade these surreal moments for anything in the world. By giving to others, YOU are the one, who receives the greater blessing!

That baby is now probably married with children of her own; I know my twins are, although only one of them has children at this time. Time flies by before we know it. We still pray for God to work through us every day, if there is another need we can help fulfill. We always try to remain sensitive, so that at any given time, we can convey God's love and become His hands and feet to our world. I believe He is going to empower us to help many this coming year.

*You don't know who may need your help, strength, or compassion; however, Jesus does, and He sees **your** willingness to answer His call. Keep your heart and mind open, because you never know what day He will order YOUR steps to become someone else's miracle. His ways are so amazing! Days like this will warm your heart for a lifetime. Psalms 34:8 "Oh taste* *and see that the Lord is good"...because He is!*

IF God Could Do It for Me, He Could Do It for Perry

~~~~~~

We moved to the little town of Harrington about eleven years ago. Since that time, we have made very many wonderful friends. It's a small town, where we feel reasonably comfortable sitting on our front porch, with only a hook lock on the screen door. Plus, we are familiar with most of our close neighbors.

One friend, in particular, we have had the pleasure of meeting, is Mrs. Kenton. She is relatively old and lives only a few houses away. She has a very sweet special needs child, who is about fifty years old. His name is Perry; however, I don't know the story behind his disability. I heard he had received some type of head injury as a baby that left him with the ability to function at a six to eight year old level.

He is such a sweet man, whom everyone in our community loves. He tells my husband, "Pat's my girlfriend!" Together, Glenn and I just smile.

We host many yard sales on our property. Family and friends love the busy location, and our Perry comes to each one of them. He likes to look over each item, and asks the price of each and every one of them. He really enjoys it. I always plant something on the table I can give him for free. Once he finds his free treasure for the day, he heads back up the street to his home, a happy camper.

At first, his worried Mom called me to make sure he was supposed to take the item. Once she understood what I was doing, she stopped. Perry simply enjoys his treasure hunts and returns home with his "bargain". Once the yard sale is over, we don't see much of our Perry, until the next person wants to have one in our yard.

One day, early on a Saturday evening, as we sat down to dinner, someone knocked on our front door. Glenn answered it and, to our surprise, it was Perry! He had never ventured up on our porch to knock on our door before. Perry came to ask how I was doing. Glenn told him I was getting much better, and he was happy to hear that news and left to return home.

I had recently gone through hip replacement surgery, and I had to return to the hospital three times in two months. The first time, of course, was for the actual operation. The next two times, they discovered I had a severe bleed, and it had formed a clot the size of at least a pint of blood, which had to be removed immediately. So that Friday, I had same day surgery, and went home late in the afternoon.

They called me AGAIN on Sunday, instructing me to return to the hospital, as soon as possible. The test results were back, my leg had become infected! So, now they wanted to insert a "Pic Line" in my arm to run continuous antibiotics for eight weeks! UGH! Away we went again! This time, I was readmitted for five additional days. My physicians tried several different antibiotics, until they found one that my body could tolerate. After my discharge, Glenn had to administer my medication through the line, every six hours around the clock. I'm telling you, this man became quite a nurse!

After about six weeks, with each dose of medication Glenn put in my pic line, I was feeling worse. I finally said, "Glenn, I feel so weak, I can feel my life *ebbing away from me." I had broken out in hives all over my back and had been fighting a high fever for over a twenty-four hour period. About six o'clock that evening, Glenn said, "We need to get you back to the hospital!"*

My immediate answer was "NO! I'm too tired! We can go in the morning." But he refused to listen. My only choice was the car, or an ambulance. I am known to be bullheaded, but I knew he meant it. I had no intention of making a spectacle of myself, by being carried out the front door on a stretcher and into an ambulance. Therefore, if I had to crawl, I would somehow get to the car.

When we arrived, it seemed we waited forever to be seen by a physician, but it was actually only two and a half hours. After we finally were taken back for treatment, the nurse assigned to my case was NOT very kind to me. I felt like she thought I was faking my illness.

When they questioned why I thought something was wrong, I explained, "Each time Glenn put that medication in my line, it felt like the muscles in my neck and across my chest were tearing, or more like they were "shredding apart". It caused me much discomfort. I continued to explain, "I don't know why, but I thought maybe he was running it too fast; however, he was only running one drop every two seconds." To help her better understand, I told her, "First, he flushes the line with saline, and then adjusts the drip from the bag. He flushes the line with Heparin twice a day, to keep it running freely."

At this point, the nurse on duty barked very curtly, "That's nonsense! I just flushed that line, and did that hurt you?" My answer was, "No, actually it didn't! I don't know why it happens...only that it does!" She adamantly replied, "**There is nothing wrong with that pic line!**"

It was at this point; the Doctor perceived her attitude and spoke up. He said, "It would do that if she was allergic to the antibiotic!" I was so glad he shut her down so quickly! I knew it wasn't my imagination, and I don't like people, who try to make me feel like I'm unintelligent! I came to find out later; the pic line that was threaded under my skin, emptied out into my body at the exact location I felt the "shredding sensation". I finally had an explanation for my excruciating pain!

Perhaps this nurse was exhausted, and feeling a bit mean. Because, when she began to put in my IV, she placed it on the inside bone of my wrist. I asked her if that was the only site it could be inserted; she assured me, even though it was very painful, it was the best place to put it. I knew in my heart, it was **NOT!** I have had many IV's in my lifetime and no one had ever placed one there. In my past, before I met Jesus, I would have handled this quickly, but I was trying to keep my temper intact. I was too sick for a scene. That was her good fortune.

I knew by now, her mean spirit was intentional and targeted directed toward me. I quietly prayed to myself asking Jesus to help me forgive her, because my flesh wanted to rise up! I am a Christian, but I still have a "Bit of the Irish" in me, too!

I will admit, I did pray that God would talk to her heart, and make her regret the way she was treating me, and to help me maintain my Christianity. I did not want to lose my temper, nor my integrity.

So, I began to tell her about the books I had

written. I shared a couple of the stories; the presence of God came into that emergency room cubicle, and she began to weep. She realized how evil she had been to me. She hugged me at least three times! I knew she would feel that sting of regret all night long!

At this time, I was too tired and sick to want anything but rest, and peace. Revenge was not on the menu. It would take a long time to tell all that happened to me. I have touched on some things in another story. I will just say I was in that hospital three times, in two months; each time I was fighting for my life. This third time was NOT a good beginning! I was being admitted because of the allergic reaction to the antibiotic. It caused my blood count to drop extremely low and I had to have a transfusion. This loss of blood is also the reason I felt like my life was ebbing away... it truly was! They told me my body was trying to fight the allergy so hard, it rapidly depleted my blood supply. They were thankful they found it in time!

So, from June eighth, until October, I hardly left my chair. Each day, I walked back and forth, throughout my home, attempting to regain my strength. Other than "angel space", that protected me from a near accident, this illness was the closest to dying I had ever come! I will tell you, if it had not been for the prayers of my wonderful church, my loving family, and praying friends, I would have died! I am glad God heard each one of them and answered!

My husband, Glenn was the new chief cook and bottle washer. He took such good care of me; I don't know what I would have done without him. Our church sent endless meals, cards, and made phone calls to check in on us. All in all, I think it took me almost a year to feel my normal self again. Now... this brings me back to Perry.

I was starting to recuperate from all of this the Saturday evening Perry came to our door. We were both so touched he was thinking about my health. I guess he had heard about my problem from his Mother.

The next morning, Glenn had gone to the Milford Memorial Hospital Intensive Care Unit, to pray for a sweet lady, who lived in the assisted living home and attended the Sunday service he held there. The other members of his worship group told him she had been admitted to the hospital and she was not doing very well.

At this time, he had been preaching this Sunday morning service for almost eighteen years. Every couple of years his class changed a little, as the Lord called some of them Home. They loved the Lord, and they came to love Glenn. Many residents remained faithful in their attendance until their end.

Because I was still a little weak, I stayed home that Sunday morning. My phone rang; it was Perry's Mother. She had just returned from the Milford Hospital I.C.U. unit herself. Right after he left our home checking on MY health, our sweet Perry had a stroke! I felt terrible! It all added up; Perry showed up on our porch because he knew something was wrong. But didn't know how to convey it to us! My heart was broken!

She asked me if we could pray for her son, and of course, I told her we would. She said, "I sat there all night with him, because they told me he was dying, and he would not make it through the next twenty-four hours. But I had to come home for a short while, to try to get some rest."

It was at this moment, I remembered Glenn was already at the hospital! I told her I would call her right back. By the time I reached him; he had just left the I.C.U. and was headed toward the elevator. I informed him of Perry's stroke and the graveness of his condition. Immediately, Glenn agreed to go back to the unit and pray for him. I called Perry's Mom and reassured her, at that very moment, my husband was on his way to Perry's bedside.

Glenn and I returned to the hospital that night, and Perry was laying there awake! His Mom said, "He woke up, but he can't speak, or eat; still, I think he knows me."

I stepped over to the bed, and even though he couldn't speak, I knew, he recognized me! After all, I was his girlfriend! Glenn and I prayed again. Once more, JESUS stepped into the room! In our hearts, we knew our boy was going to live! Each day he showed significant signs of improvement, and he began eating pureed food. When he spoke out asking for some "real food," we all shared a hearty laugh! Within a week, Perry was home and doing well, but we didn't see him out walking anymore after that.

Time moved on; before we knew it, summer appeared and once again it was yard sale season. That weekend, as usual, a couple of families got together to host a yard sale out front. As they finished setting up, I glanced up and could not believe who I saw walking down the street! It was our Perry!

He sauntered up to the tables and yelled, "Hey, PAT! How much is this? Pat! How much is this one?" until he finally found his deal. "Hey, Pat, how much is this one?" I smiled from my porch, and said, "Perry, this is your lucky day! That one is free, just for you."

As he walked home to show off his new treasure, I could see our boy was as happy as ever. However, I think the payoff was really mine. I don't think he could have possibly felt any better than I did, right at that moment. I was sick, and Jesus pulled me through. I knew if He could do it for me, He could do it for Perry! Yes! "HE" sure did!

He Who Dwells In the Secret Place
~~~~~~

   I have read in **Psalms 91:1, "He that dwelleth in the secret place of the most High shall abide under the shadow of the Almighty."** *This is a remarkable promise given to us by God! As I began to think deeply about these words, so many beautiful thoughts began to flood my mind. What would it be like to dwell in the shadow of God? Just think about it. Would we see many more miraculous things happen, when we pray? My mind continued to ponder on this thought. To be that close to someone would mean he would see and hear everything I did or said. Would I be good enough?*

   I asked myself, how would it be possible for me to dwell that close to God? I'd never live up to it; I make too many mistakes in a day. He would know every move I made and each thought I was thinking. I defeated my own argument; because He is God...He already knows it all. That surely can't be it; so could the secret place actually be a "thing" or some physical place?

   As I contemplated these thoughts, it HIT me! To "dwell" there, was not for Him to know me better, but for ME to understand and know HIM better. That was it! The Bible says in Jeremiah, 1:5, "Before I formed thee in the belly I knew thee." I have read about it, sang about it, and at this moment, I am writing about it, asking Him to direct my every word. All this time, Jesus was simply inviting me to develop an intimate and personal relationship with Him. I believe the "secret place" is prayer; and when we fall on our knees, accepting His call to come before the Mercy Seat and into the Holiest of Holies, the shadow of the Almighty covers us all day long. James 4:8 says, "Draw nigh unto God, and He will draw nigh to you..." He will reveal Himself, and give us revelation of things we never knew before. It is the place we will discover things we need to rid from our fleshly nature. He will comfort us, help us find our way, and give us strength to continue on our spiritual journey. This Savior of ours never intended for one soul to be lost! He desires each of us to make it to that City Of Gold! However, His plan was to grant us a "choice"....if we want to dwell in Heaven with Him for eternity, we must live our lives the way He desires, while here on earth. The sacrifice God asks of us, to live holy, does not even begin to compare to the price He paid, to make our salvation possible.

As hard as I strive, I fail daily. Every day, when I can't think of one thing I have done wrong, in the secret place on bended knee, I ask forgiveness. Truthfully, I know there has never been one day of my life, that I have been perfect! Please keep in mind, as long as I remain in my very opinionated flesh that may never happen! The Bible says in Isaiah 64:6 ... "Our righteousness is as filthy rags,... Still, this does not excuse me from trying to do my very best.

Now, let's consider the "secret place" and the "Shadow of the Almighty". When the sun rises, our human shadow is very long. This means I can walk side by side with my companion, remain a distance away, and with no fear of bumping into Him, I can continue to walk in His shadow. Could this be symbolic of precious time spent in prayer, before the best hour of our day is consumed by others? As the afternoon wears on, our shadow shortens in length. Thus, I would have to walk **extremely** close in order to dwell in His shadow. In the spiritual realm, no matter what time of day, *PRAYER allows us to live in His presence!* How can we abide? If our spirit is keen, we will always find somewhere or somehow to reach out to others. Can you make a phone call to someone you know, who is discouraged or depressed? You have the power to pray with them right there on the telephone and leave them with encouraging words of wisdom. Perhaps someone you know is facing a terrible trial; a card in their mailbox can make all the difference! Can you prepare a meal for someone ill or elderly? Do you know a young Mother, who simply needs a two hour break from it all? These little things, which seem very insignificant to you, may mean the world to someone else at this moment.

My oldest daughter is a very busy Mama, too. She home schools two small ones and has two in college. I called her and told her I had prepared an extra pan of lasagna for their dinner; she was thrilled to receive it! These are the kindnesses that encourage the heart and spirit; it physically says, "I love you!"

These gestures of love are not only for my family. Whenever the need is presented, I do them throughout my community. Cooking a meal for someone in need, allows ME to receive a bigger blessing, than I could hope to give. Do these service gifts please God? I believe they do. I believe He writes them all down. That is not the reason I do them; I simply want to be a blessing to others.

I think all of these things are important to God's kingdom. If you are aware of a need, and you can help... DO IT! Many times, as we have shaken a hand, we have palmed a twenty dollar bill. Sometimes we simply knew they could use it; other times one of us just felt a nudge *from the Lord. No matter WHY we did it, seeing their countenance light up and hearing a sign of relief escape their lips was worth so much more! Once, God used us to provide gas for someone in great need. The warmth that filled our hearts was our reward. Another time, a full bag of unexpected groceries given to someone, who had no idea what they would prepare for their children's dinner, made all the difference in the world for that family.*

Why don't you try praying for God to direct your day? Desiring to be in His perfect will, I have done this many times and found His plan was very different from mine. I will tell you when you realize what just occurred; it fills your heart with so much joy. When you comprehend, "Today, God used ME", it is a beautiful "Ah Ha" moment. Just knowing He answered your prayer and guided you all the day long, will leave you amazed. Don't be afraid to ask; for He will take care of you. When you get there, He will already be there waiting to help you. I believe this is one of those "under the shadow" places.

Have you ever made an unplanned stop in your vehicle, to answer an unexpected phone call? At that moment, it may have annoyed you. However, as you continued your journey, just a few miles down the road, you realized the horrible accident at the intersection COULD have been YOU! We may not give much thought to these things, BUT GOD saw ahead of time and changed the enemies plan to destroy you! Perhaps, just two minutes saved your life! Could it be we were spared, because in the early hours of our day, we found time to dwell in His shadow? Could it be in our humanity we did not realize just how closely the

Shepherd watches over us? Many times, after an experience like this, we suddenly comprehend the magnitude of the miracle that just occurred. Things like this happened to me many times; because He loved me before I knew Him, His plan for my life remained intact.

Have you ever felt His presence so close, you thought if you opened your eyes you might actually SEE Him? I have. I was in the sanctuary with my husband, Glenn. Andy, our son, who had just got off from work as a prison guard, and John, a police officer, who attends our church, met us for a time of prayer.

Our Pastor's daughter had just been diagnosed with a severe illness and we decided to meet every night at twelve thirty. John and Andy both worked the evening shifts; and although John could not be there every night, because his shifts would change weekly, he came whenever he could. That man knew how to come against the gates of hell! Together... we were warriors; we purposed to come against any sickness trying to harm our Pastor's family. With the exception of regular service nights, on Wednesday and Sunday, we continued this prayer schedule for fourteen weeks. I tell you, the very first night we prayed, a haze filled the sanctuary! We all witnessed it. Although it was very early in the morning, He let us know He was right there with us. We were standing on His promises; with every ounce of strength within us, all we wanted was to do His will.

Have you ever spent the night at the bedside of a sick friend or family member? Maybe you have ministered in any capacity you could, to comfort a dying friend. When we become His hands and His feet to a hurting world, we must be in His shadow.

These are all my own opinions, but I feel anything

we do for God brings us into His presence. If we have first spent time praying and asking Him to lead our day, He will not let us down.

We should bring our flesh under subjection and be willing to work, pray, and love, souls into His kingdom. For example, without prayer as my first priority, I could not even begin to write this story. I asked the Lord to place a subject on my heart and anoint me to convey His message in a way that will bless someone else. I am not a typist.. every word is hunt and peck. Within my limited ability, there is no way I could accomplish the task of writing a book! All along the way Jesus has helped me; I have actually gained tremendous speed! A real typist may disagree to this statement, but it is a high speed, compared to the way I began. What He has lead me to do is amazing, and I will continue to earnestly listen for my next spiritual assignment. I want to be a willing vessel. Like everyone else, at times I royally mess up! I fail greatly; but I fall on my knees and, once again, I ask forgiveness. Jesus always provides me with the strength to pick up the broken pieces. I set my face like a flint and keep moving forward.

What a privileged way to live! I am aware of no other place on earth that will give me peace in my heart and mind, for NO ONE loves me like He does. He will allow me to walk in His shadow, through every valley and storm of life. My Pastor has always pointed out the words in Psalms 23 which says, "Yea though I walk **through** *the valley of the shadow of death..." That simply means we will not remain there forever. As long as we allow Jesus to lead us, we WILL come out on the victory side! Learn to trust him; He will never lead you* *wrong.*

If we are going to make Heaven our home, why not make up our minds to take a few more with us? Develop a personal relationship with God; every day ask Him to order your steps, and then trust that He knows exactly where He is directing you and why. Believe me once you begin living in the secret place of prayer, you will desire to "dwell in the shadow of the Almighty .... forever!"

As I finished this story, I asked my Glenn what was his take on the Shadow of the Almighty? He said "A shadow has an influence; it covers, protects, and invites rest!" I think that pretty well sums it up, and needed to be put in print, don't you?

God Said, "Go Home Now! Ashley Needs You!"

~~~~~~~~~~~~~~~~~~~~~~~~~~~~~~~~~~~~~

Glenn and I decided to go to the grocery store before his four to twelve work shift began. Because of my horrible back situation, this would enable him to carry the groceries in for me. He has always taken excellent care of me that way. Even though he knew he had a full night's work ahead of him; it never seemed to matter to him at all. He has always been my handsome prince, even to this day. I admit it, I am spoiled, and loving it!

God has blessed me greatly with this wonderful man. When I went through the worst years of my life, God made me a promise Joel 2:25 that I will restore the years the canker worm had eaten... He kept that promise and blessed me immensely with the love and kindness of this wonderful man. We are so blessed and I look forward to many more beautiful years together.

It was a beautiful, early spring day. I don't remember why Ashley, our youngest daughter, was home from school that day, but she was. She was about fifteen, and well able to stay home by herself. She had done so, many times, and we were both comfortable with it. As we were walking through the store, we had placed several purchases in the cart. Thank God, none were perishable, as I usually shop that aisle last. All of a sudden, the voice of God spoke to me. All He said was, "Go home now! Ashley needs you!" It literally sent a jolt through my body! By the shocked look on my face, Glenn knew something was terribly wrong. I told him what God had spoken to me. Without hesitation, we left the cart sitting right in the isle, and almost ran for the car!

69

For the most part, I am not an easily frightened person, but such a fear gripped my heart; I sensed danger was near. While we drove through downtown breaking the speed limit, I began praying. We were approximately ten minutes away; thankfully, it was a straight path to our house.

As we approached our driveway, there stood a grungy looking young man, with his foot planted in OUR front door. He was preventing Ashley from closing it! From the driveway, I could see her fingers wrapped around the door edge from the inside, trying to hold it so he could not get it opened any further.

As we were pulling up beside the porch, I put my window down and very curtly said, "Can I help you?" Basically, I was serving notice, the Cavalry had just arrived!

I think our quick unexpected arrival into the driveway caught him off guard, and shook him up a bit. The dust from our dirt driveway was flying everywhere, as Glenn threw the car into park. Jerking to a stop, he jumped out and headed for the porch.

The man began to stammer, "UH, I was just trying to see if she wanted to buy this cleaning product." There was a spray bottle in his hand; however, it was NOT a labeled, cleaning product!

We advised him we were not interested in anything he had to sell, and told him to leave our front porch immediately! I was very angry and spoke harshly, "How dare you! Why did you put your foot in my front door in the first place? Who do you think you are? We saw you preventing our daughter from closing the door."

We fired one question after another so fast, it threw him off guard. The man was looking around *searching for a way to get past us and get out of there.*

I was shaking from fright. Since this stranger never offered a sales pitch of what he was supposedly selling, I think he knew he had better exit quickly, before his true intentions became clearer to us. Mama and Papa bear were in full view, and I believe he did not want to linger long! He practically ran off our front porch, and never looked back. Were we angry? Yes! But, I believe God, Himself, held us back and gave us authority over the spiritual darkness in this young man.

I couldn't help but think he had other intentions in his mind, or why would God have spoken those words to me in the market? I was just relieved; Glenn and I were able to get between him, and our sweet baby girl.

I will tell you, if you purpose to hurt me, that is one thing. I may put up a resistance, but you get to live. However, if you come to hurt one of my children; it is a whole different story, and it tends to bring mama bear out. That is a side of me, I don't even like!

I am not saying my children are above discipline, and correction. If they do wrong, I will stand in agreement with you, and take care of it. On the other hand, I will not uphold violence or scare tactics directed at my children. The atmosphere will change very quickly. I know all you loving and protective Mama's can relate to what I am saying.

Our would-be intruder was not too happy with us. The attitude he displayed, as we watched him leave, made it evident. We went inside quickly and shut the door behind us.

Now, I am sure you know, the first question I asked Ashley was, "Why did you open the door to that stranger? You know we have always instructed you

NEVER to open the door for a stranger!" Her reply was, "He knocked on the door just like you do, Mom. I thought you must have forgotten something and came back." I always used the tune, "shave and a haircut, two bits" knock. This man had used that same knock, and she assumed her Dad and I had returned. Who would have ever thought, such a coincidence like this would happen? Or, is it possible he had watched our habits for a while, from a distance? I guess we will never know.

For the record, I have never used that knock again. Ashley told us, as soon as she opened the door and realized it was not us, she tried to shut it; but he stuck his foot in the door to prevent her from getting it closed.

It terrified her to see the position that she was in! Knowing we were not due back from grocery shopping any time soon, she was alone and had no way of protecting herself. But when you have praying parents, who plead the blood of Jesus, over their children, and their home, He does watch out for them. There is no telling what could have happened, had we arrived only five minutes later! Even now, I shudder to think about it! While we were out of reach, God was right there watching over our girl.

Glenn went back outside a few minutes later, and found a significant "X "marked on one our front steps. He felt like it was that man's doing, and he had marked our home for some specific reason. Glenn immediately washed it off and soon afterward left for work.

I am so thankful for all the benefits God provides, when we serve Him. I know bad things happen to good people, and I have experienced that, too. Still, for the most part, I place my trust in Him to keep us safe. I know I can call, and in moments, He will hear me and answer. I spend time every day, talking to Him in prayer. I want the Lord, to recognize my voice, in any situation. Knowing He does, brings great comfort to me. Walk with Jesus, trust your instincts, learn to recognize the sound of His voice, and stay tuned to it for instructions. If you stay close to him, and trust in His Word, your steps will be directed. Had I not recognized His voice, that day could have ended much differently. I thank Him for the miracle He performed that day! Pleading the blood of Jesus over our home and family every morning really pays! I wouldn't give up these incredible benefits for anything in the world! It is unfortunate that some do. BUT, like Joshua 24:15 says, **"As for me and my house we will serve the Lord!"**

Facing the Winds of Adversity

~~~~~~~~~~~~~~~~~~~~~~~~~~~~~~~~~~~~~

　　I have faced many trials in my lifetime, none of which have been easy for me. Adversity is not easy for **anyone.** *If I were to take a survey of all those who are reading this book, I could safely conclude at some point in life, most everyone has had to deal with circumstances, which have caused them conflict or great pain.*

　　Humanity has a tendency to always believe the old adage, "The grass is always greener on the other side of the fence." The poverty stricken believe the wealthy have no problems; their money solves everything. How could they possibly understand the terror of receiving an eviction notice or a sleepless night of anguish, knowing there is nothing for breakfast in the morning! They may have a few ups and downs, but they do not have a clue what it is like to be poor! On the other hand, the wealthy many times surmise the poverty stricken certainly have their share of problems; however they are nothing in comparison to the issues we face on a daily basis. At least they have the freedom of being themselves; they have true friends...not those that just want what they can get from them! My children are engulfed in sports, my husband is never home.. a family meal. What is that? We may live in a beautiful house, but I would give anything for a home. They believe my money takes care of it all. The truth is, somehow we **all** *believe our situation is the most dire; and in the heat of the moment, that may be so.*

　　Sadness comes to all of us. No matter what our status in life, at times, it seems devastation and

*heartache lurks around every corner, waiting to greet us
with the morning sun. The list of situations that produce
gaping wounds in our hearts is endless. Perhaps you
have faced the death of a loving parent, spouse, or
extended family member, which has left a lingering
feeling of loss and drained your emotions. Sometimes, we
simply mourn the loss of wasted time we could have
spent with someone we loved, which can never be
retrieved. There is a loss of valuable things, such as
homes, vehicles, jobs, investments, meaningful
relationships and friendships. What about deep inward
painful situations? Like those caused by the betrayal of a
spouse or trusted friend...perhaps you have suffered
physical and emotional abuse, and have felt the knife
wrenching cut of slander and jealousy, that has left you
feeling as though something has been stolen and can
never be replaced.*

*I think you understand where I am headed.
Should a reader survey be taken, I feel assured many
would relate to three or more of these circumstances;
and perhaps, at some point in YOUR life, you have faced
every one of them. If not, brace yourself! I am not being
negative; it is simply a fact of life. You will face hard, life
changing storms. Whether you are in one at this
particular moment, or simply cannot overcome what has
happened in the past, my desire is to try to help you
work through your pain.*

*The winds of trial and adversity sometimes
blow so hard, we can barely stand; we feel as though
we will never be able to hold our head high again. Prayer
is the best path you can take; for God is Sovereign and
He will never leave you alone! Although there will be
times you feel your earnest pleas have gone no farther*

than the ceiling of your prayer room and inevitably bounced right back in your face, rest assured your Heavenly Father heard every word. Not only that, but the Bible says He stores every tear you shed in a vial and your prayers are always before Him. There were days I thought I would die, because the horrible gulf between the prayers and the answer seemed endless. At times, tears were the only prayers I could pray, but the Lord understood my heart. In my lifetime, I have prayed for God to take vengeance on the one who hurt my children so deeply it was beyond words....but He did not. I thought dear Jesus, whose side are you on? Still, I received no answer; Heaven was SILENT! I know this may seem strange coming from the lips of a Christian, but keep in mind, just because I author books, I am not flawless. I am simply being as open and honest as I can, to enable you to understand we are all human flesh. We must be patient and hold on to our faith, knowing one day there WILL be an answer to our questions!

I felt alone... as though no one else could have possibly endured this much trauma; at least not the kind I had been dealt. Up to this point in my life, I had faced many harrowing situations, but none of them came close to comparing to the heartache I was facing at this particular time. I was completely broken, both mentally and physically. The ache in my heart was so great; some days it was a struggle to breath! I wanted God to immediately avenge me of every adversary. I was so broken, I thought surely God would bring His wrath and take care of those who tore my world apart, but He didn't. I truly had a hard time understanding this. You see, in the midst of the storm, our vision is distorted and our perspective is completely out of alignment with the

Word of God...He is Love....and in His great wisdom, handles everything HIS way. I know there are many of you, who can relate to the personal misery I am speaking of, for you have encountered similar circumstances.

It took a lot of prayer on my part to keep moving forward. For the sake of my children, I had to make a personal choice to set my face like a flint; I wanted them to feel safe and know we were all going to be alright. I stayed busy with my new one parent family and continued to remain involved with most of our church functions; this helped me to stay encouraged and strengthened my walk with the Lord. It wasn't until later; I actually began to realize just how much God was protecting my every step!

Time moved on; but there was never one day I didn't have to continually look over my shoulder to make sure my former spouse was not lying in wait to harm me or my children. Even after nineteen long years went by, I still received threatening phone calls and suffered untold mental torment.

For example, I had been remarried for seventeen years, when during the night, the air conditioner downstairs, was partially moved; someone had tried to take it out of the window. Luckily, when Glenn installed it, he attached it to the window sill with very long screws. Someone would have had to actually break the window to remove it! I was so glad Glenn had thought of that. It worked! I thank God for His protection.

Two years later, I received a call from one of his counselors urging me "to beware"; He was in yet another rage! My inner alarm was already on full alert; for God had warned me he was in a crazed frame of mind! Again,

I prayed for the safety of my family. I could NOT imagine why Jesus, in His greatness, did not step in and once and for all remove the continuing threat! It had become such a thorn in my flesh. Still, I had no answer to my question; yet I knew God was protecting me.... because I was still alive!

After his death, I was told by one of his psychologists, he had followed me and the children everywhere we went for two years, except to church! He related to his counselor he knew I sensed his presence in every parking lot. He watched, as I circled the parking lot making sure his truck was nowhere to be seen. Once I stepped out of my car, he watched me scan the area before I allowed my children to exit the vehicle. He laughed as he divulged borrowing a friend's car so I would not see him; yet, he knew I could feel his spirit. It was a cat and mouse game to him. I shuddered to hear this, because that was exactly what I did! How would he have known my actions, had he not been watching me?

At the time; I resided in a small bungalow nestled behind a mansion. The owner had previously installed an alarm system that alerted him of any vehicle or pedestrian, who entered the gate on his private half mile long driveway. Therefore, when a restraining order was placed against my ex, I finally had a sense of security. I provided him with a description of my ex- husband's vehicle, and my landlord knew to call 911 at the first sight of him.

We had a local poultry processing plant in our city. The back of their parking lot adjoined to a twenty acre field which, at this time was planted with corn. Unfortunately, it also formed the property line just behind my residence. I was informed he parked in their lot, ran through twenty acre corn field, and watched us through the windows! He told his counselor he knew my son and I could sense he was nearby, because as night approached, Wayne would nervously look out the back window of his room towards the edge of the planted field. My ex knew my son must have relayed this to me, for soon after, I appeared, closed the windows, pulled the curtains, locked the doors, and turned on the air conditioner. Unless he truly saw us, how else could he have known our actions?

With hope in my heart I'd say, "Wayne, Daddy is not out there; the landlord would have heard him come up the driveway or certainly would have seen him walking, because the alarm would have alerted him. I think we are just easily spooked, because of all we have been through." Of course, it never crossed my mind my ex would gain access to my home through that huge cornfield! Yet, after the children were safely tucked in bed, I felt an uneasiness lingering in the air that convinced me he truly was close by. As I write this, I still shudder...but I also know without a doubt, God protected me, even more then I realized back then! He hid this from me; for He knew if I had known for sure it was more than our imaginations... that my ex really WAS out there, I could have never fallen asleep.

There were many nights, after we had said bedtime prayers, Wayne said, "I'm afraid, Mom!" I wanted to scoop him up and carry him to my bedroom, with me and Amy, to let him sleep on a pallet of quilts. I had to force myself to leave him in his own room. I knew he had to learn to deal with his fears through prayers. Sometimes we had to pray together several times until he felt the assurance he needed. The doorway to my room was only about ten feet from his. I always left the bathroom light on, which lit the entire bungalow and his door open in case he needed me. I promised I would "sleep lightly" in order to hear any disturbance and protect him. I NEVER let him know how afraid I truly was; as a Mother, I only longed to comfort this frightened little boy, who was becoming a man way too soon. No child should EVER have to go through experiences like this! No matter how I felt, I had to present a strong stance for my children.

Nights were the worst. I continually listened for any strange sound. My body was always on full alert. As I tried to sleep, I had to literally talk myself a muscle at a time into relaxing! It was a horrible way to live! Many times only the security of the sun rise, allowed deep sleep, until the alarm clock sounded or the kids woke me up.

Time moved on; I met Glenn about two years later. We were happily married and now had four children. While I still received "warning calls" on occasion, there was not a day I stepped out of my door without scanning my surroundings. I was continually on my guard. God continued to protect our family.

One day, out of the blue, things changed! I received a call from my Pastor requesting that Glenn and I to meet with him after service, on Sunday evening. We could not begin to figure out what he wanted to discuss with us, and our imaginations began to work over time. Had I said something to offend someone? At this time, we were facing extreme financial difficulty and my nerves were frayed; so I thought it was possible. However, it was a much bigger issue that completely shocked both of us! It had to do with a matter I vaguely *mentioned in one of my previous books.*

My former husband, the man who had tormented us all these years, had received a horrible diagnosis. At the most, he had only a few months to live. He called our Pastor desiring to once again become a member of our church. Our Pastor told him he would pray, and present it to Glenn and me. He would never tell anyone they could not attend the church; but my Pastor also knew the terrible situation this could create. He knew we had invested our lives in this church; and he understood my ex's return may cause us to feel we needed to find a new place of worship. He, of all people, knew firsthand the trauma our family had gone through in the previous years, and all we endured. Even though the two oldest were now married, it could have set their own nerves on edge once again.

Because we still had the twins at home at this time, he did not want us to feel we had to pack up and run, taking them away from the support of their school and church friends, like I used to have to do, before I married Glenn. I was always trying to find a safer place to live.

This wonderful man of God sitting before us, conveyed the request he had received and never once tried to influence our decision. With all we had been through, he understood this had to be our decision and ours alone. He made it very clear whatever we decided, he would certainly stand beside us. He would never turn anyone away from salvation, but we knew he could recommend another church nearby of our same faith.

Of course, the reason for this meeting came as a complete shock to both of us! At first, we didn't know what to think or say. Immediately, my two oldest children came to my mind. I thought to myself, "Surely, this man's short time left on earth will probably help his children forgive him. IF he is truly repentant and gets his life together." I comforted myself it would only be for a very short time. He only had a few weeks to live; we could do this for our children's sake!

We openly discussed the situation with our Pastor; there was only one decision we could possibly make... Glenn and I agreed to allow him to come back. He needed the opportunity to make his heart right with God. We would not stand between ANYONE and the cross.... especially not a lost dying soul!

*He and his new wife returned to church; God touched him in such a miraculous way. He went into remission and lived another FIVE years! The Lord knew it was best I did not perceive He would grant this man these quality years, for I would not have been able to fathom walking on eggshells for such a long period of time. It was still very stressful; I took one day at a time, hoping and praying he would keep himself together. I had reached a point he could no longer penetrate **my** mind, but I don't think I could have taken one more slap on my children's hearts! We simply trusted God and kept moving forward, praying every day for God's protection, wisdom and direction...daily He granted us **Grace!***

During this time, he was just as up and down in his moods as he had always been, but God knew what He was doing; I was sure of that! We certainly were not the best of buddies by any stretch of the imagination. Once, I did try to shake both of their hands, it did not go too well, for I ended up experiencing nightmares for a week! I learned to keep my distance and pleasantly smile, or nod my head. Occasionally in passing, I would politely speak, "I hope you are doing well with your treatments." Looking back, I can't believe we had the strength to do it! I do know, without Jesus helping us, it would not have been possible.

Even though I agreed to do this, it was far from easy. I prayed, "Dear Jesus, if you take him, please don't let the kids even think he died lost!" They knew the life this man had lived for the past twenty years or more. They remembered the horror that ravaged our home. But they also knew what it meant if he did not get his heart right with the Lord. I did not want to allow roots of bitterness and hatred to dwell in their tender hearts! He had to be forgiven by all of us!

So once again, Mama, with the help and grace of Jesus Christ and with the love and steadfastness of my husband, Glenn, took the first steps to walk a path back to Calvary for all of us. Even though at times all I felt was numbness, I did what I knew was right in God's sight.... always praying for the best.

The kids were actually able to establish a good relationship with him. Yes, they were cautious, because during their childhood, they formed very few good times and I was thankful, during this fairly stable time in his life, they were actually able to laugh and make some lasting memories to hold on to. Now that they were adults, I prayed he would not do anything to ruin this last opportunity for this precious time together. I had confidence they were well able to handle themselves, should any conflicting circumstances arise. There were a few bumps in the road, and I was very proud of the way they handled each one.

His remission was now over, and the last few weeks of his life, the two of his children took loving care of him. It was absolutely amazing to see what God had done...they didn't "Forget" ...but they "Forgave!" They buried their biological Father believing he went through heavens gates; I believe he made it, too. When we worship around the throne together, we will never have to be afraid again! After everyone had left the funeral service, my Pastor spoke to me. He said, "I have never seen such forgiveness in my entire life!" I quickly put my hand up to stop him and replied, "Whoa, I have to be very honest. Please don't pin any roses on me. I didn't do it for him; I did it for my children!" His heartfelt words were, "I don't care who you did it for, and the fact is... you did it!"

He made me cry that day; it was okay... no matter what the reason... I still did it! It erased the feeling of guilt; for somehow, because it was for the sake of my children, I thought it didn't really count. Parent's do a lot of things for their children they couldn't do for anyone else, and Glenn and I were no different. When someone hurts your children, they have to go through you! An inward alarm automatically goes off and you will protect them at any cost!

*I have since spoken to another one of his psychologists; He was able to help me understand the underlying causes of his erratic behavior; hearing it made sense. It helped explain the "whys" and answered many of the questions I held in my heart for so long. For years, I lived with the accusation it was **my entire fault;** the counselor assured me it was not. As a very young man, things spoken into his life molded his character to behave the way he did; so it wasn't his entire fault either. Parent's, PLEASE, be very careful of the words you speak to your children; they are more powerful than*

*you think! They will believe you! Words we speak build
or break our impressionable children. YOU have the
power to set the direction of their lives towards failure or
success.*

*I was the recipient of the words that had been
spoken in his life. I endured his anger and rage for
literal years, and suffered at his hands. Many times in
panic, I gathered my two children, hoping and praying
he would not kill us, as we ran for our lives! This was
reality... not just imagined fears. His Psychiatrist called
me late one night saying he had plans to do just that!
All I could do was suck my breath in and pray!
Immediately, my mind raced to where each of my
children was at this very moment! Glenn was at work. I
asked the Doctor, "Why? I have not spoken a word to the
man in over nineteen years!" He replied, "People like
him will tell a lie until they actually believe the story
they told. Then, they want to kill you for the lie they
believed!"*

*He continued on, telling me he could lose his
license for revealing this to me, but he could not lay his
head on his own pillow without warning me. Of course, I
would never report him; but I did comfort him by letting
him know, whenever my ex was in a rage, GOD made
me aware in my spirit! I always knew!*

*I will admit, I was silently unnerved and angry! I
was tired of fearing this man, but once again I survived.
This made me ask the Lord, "Why did you make me
endure all those harrowing years?" Why didn't you send
Your wrath and remove him?" At this moment, He began
to speak to my heart. I was typing as fast as I could, so I
would not forget it. He said, "I had to remove you and
the children from the home or he would have killed you,*

leaving them Motherless. Yet, your own prayers, asking me to not let your children know he died lost had to be answered. If he took your life, he would have died in prison with no hope of Heaven, not because I wouldn't forgive him, but because he never would have forgiven himself enough to ask Me. This way, ALL of your prayers were answered, because I loved you ALL!" I was so shocked... I could hardly breathe! I knew it was Jesus; I know His voice! I could have never had such a profound thought on my own!

As it is now, I have been healed from this particular pain. God is faithful! My oldest son from that marriage is now a minister of the Gospel, married to an earth angel, Paula, with three grown children of their own. My oldest daughter is married to a minister, raising four fine children. Glenn and I had our twins, Ashley and Andy. They are both married to partners handpicked by the Lord. They are all wonderful blessings to our lives.

Yes, I have been through the meat grinder of life, but my trust in Jesus, the ONE who brought me through each step of the storm, is stronger than ever before. I am delighted beyond words the way it all worked out for everyone, and content with the answer He gave me. I realize He didn't have to tell me "why," yet I am so thankful He did. His mercy is everlasting! It has helped me heal inwardly. I blindly trusted... not because I knew I loved Jesus... but because I knew He loved ME.

I was recently speaking to my sister about a book she was reading. The author related, when the winds of adversity blow, first check the direction of the wind; if you walk with the wind, that day it is much easier to keep walking. As my mind drifted, I thought, "GOD I

*know that would have been much easier; why didn't I
see this before?" He answered my thought right then.
"Yes, it would have been easier; and that is alright at
times. But always remember, facing the winds of a
strong storm is what it takes to fill your wings with
enough wind to fly!" If the books I have written are
never read, or if they never help anyone else in my
lifetime, it has helped ME to share these painful
memories of my past; it has helped my heart to heal,
however, I pray God has used it, dear reader, to bless
and strengthen YOU too! Try Him... most of all trust
Him... your answer is on the way! He is so good to me, I
cannot tell it all! Because of His love, patience, and
guidance, I am now finally ," On The Other Side Of
Broken" ... I hope to meet you here too!*

Don't Miss Today's Blessing Looking for Tomorrow's

~~~~~~

I have prayed not only for words of wisdom to share with you; but to empower you with something that will change your life's perspective. I long to bring joy back into your own heart, I know I am nothing within myself, but through experience, God has opened my eyes to see far beyond the moment. He has revealed the gift of seeing beyond temporary circumstances and to be genuinely grateful for each and every blessing in my life.

*Glenn and I received an incredible promise that was spoken to us almost thirty-two years ago. We continue to believe with all our hearts, it will come to pass! Yes, there have certainly been times of doubt; still, we continue to thank Him, as if it has already been fulfilled. No matter how crazy it sounds at times, "blind faith" and the fact that He said He would, is all we have in front of us! You can never sit in the seat of doubt and receive a promised blessing without faith. Even though it looks and sounds impossible, we **must choose to believe!***

According to the Word of God, doubt does not please the Lord; He does not respond to unbelief. Of course, our humanity causes each one of us to hide under the Juniper tree from time to time, as the Prophet Elijah did, while running from Jezebel for his life; still, we cannot live there! The Lord hates unbelief. It says in Hebrew 11:6, "But without faith, it is impossible to please Him...." Matthew 13:58 states, "And He did not many mighty works there because of their unbelief." Jesus refused to perform miracles in their midst, simply because they would not believe! To me it sounds as though our faith is very important to Him!

Keeping this in mind, I began to change my prayers. I asked Him to allow me to see through His eyes...to anoint my mind and give me the ability to pray in the Spirit, until I could comprehend His power and authority! I longed for understanding; I wanted to see whatever it was He needed to reveal to me, so I could walk in His perfect will.

I have great faith; I am not afraid to pray for **anything***! I have all the confidence in the world in Jesus. This is my third book relating miracles I have prayed for myself and He performed, or those I have personally witnessed. It's not as though He has not answered me in the past. With that being said, I realize, while I had no problem giving God all the glory for His marvelous acts, I still found myself very sad, waiting for our "***Significant***" promise... the promise I knew only Jesus could bring to pass. It was a huge prophecy; one that would be such a blessing! It would mean so much to so many. In prayer, I asked, "Lord, when will this promise come to pass?" At times, as I waited and then waited some more, my anxiousness would overwhelm me. Constantly, my wearied heart would ask, "God, I know it was a word from you, so why hasn't it happened yet?" As time moved on, I realized, I had to have a change of heart... if I didn't, the promise that was supposed to "bless" me would "destroy" me!*

I began to thank Him for things I had never acknowledged before, like a healthy beating heart, lungs that breathe, eyes that see, ears that still hear the simple pleasure of a child's laughter. Most people, including myself, up to this point, take these fundamental things for granted. To own a vehicle that runs well, and have money to keep gas in the tank is a blessing from Him!

I gazed around the family room, which was my prayer room most of the time. I began to realize God had blessed us with everything we possessed, from the furniture to the pictures hanging on the walls. Something so simple as the beautiful fall colors I had decorated my house with, gave me untold pleasure. A spirit of "thankfulness" gave me a warm fuzzy feeling... it was God...He was blessing my inner soul as well!

All of a sudden, all those sad times spent waiting for the promise of God to come, was replaced with a sense of peace; for I knew it would come in His perfect timing.

How could I have been so blinded by the promise that I lost the joy I could have been partaking of all those years? Now, I wait for the coming promise, in a much different state of mind; I see the beauty of each new day and anticipate the joy it will bring.

We believe the resources will come to enable us to reach the downtrodden and be a helping hand to those in need. He will empower us to help the homeless find shelter, living happily on top of life instead of clinging to the bottom! Life without Jesus has left the world destitute and so hopeless they cannot begin to see their way out. I know He will enable us to do much for His Kingdom in this area. It is our desire to show His love to a devastated world! We concluded a long time ago, that there were many who were much worse off than we were and it made us very thankful for what we have.

What about you? Perhaps it is time for you to start your change and decide to make a difference in your own life. You are the only one, who can make it happen! Become aware of the blessings you have right where you are. If you can't afford "new" things to decorate your home, visit a yard sale... colors are beautiful , even if they are purchased from a thrift shop. I have done this many times; I had no problem creating a beautiful atmosphere. As a wife, it is my God given responsibility to create a happy home ... a safe place...a haven that makes my husband and children look forward to coming home. In fact, I have been instrumental in helping new families in our church, turn their "house" into a "home". I've helped them create a happy atmosphere, and with joy flooding my heart, watched the "warm fuzzy feelings" in their hearts spread to a smile on their faces.

I could have experienced this all along. It is sad but true... I failed to see it all as a blessing from God! Keep in mind, if you ask, just like He did for me, God will help you see things differently, too. However, YOU must allow your own heart to make up its mind to count the blessings you already possess on a daily basis. Learn to appreciate the little things just as I did. A sunny day is a treasure; however, rainy days produce flowers and rainbows! There is no fragrance like the air, after a fresh rain bathes the earth. Hold a newborn baby, listen to the infectious laughter of a toddler; and see that life goes on. Dwell on the positive things in your life; no matter what you are facing...choose JOY! It is like medicine for the soul. These unique pleasures are always there and they won't cost you a dime. It is simply up to us to see them. Then, they become little blessings that feel like love.

You may say to yourself, but my promise has not yet arrived, what do I have to be happy about right now?

Allow yourself to smell the fresh cut grass, and thank God you can. Listen to the birds sing... then, thank Him again. For years, until the Lord provided the means for me to purchase a hearing aid, I could not hear their song. The first time I stepped outside onto my back porch, I stopped in my tracks! I could hear the birds singing and praising their Creator with their songs. It was the first time in seven years I had been able to hear them, and it brought tears to my eyes. It amazed me.... I didn't realize how much I missed it until God made a way to give it back.

Do you understand, if you have ten dollars in your wallet, you are richer than eighty percent of the of the world's population? Think about this surprising fact. If there is nothing in your wallet, most of us are certain Friday's paycheck is just around the corner...we know where our next dollar will be coming from. Again, eighty percent of the world's population does not! They have no idea where their next meal will come from, or where they will lay their head to rest tonight. Thank God for what you have!

Face tomorrow with a different outlook; jump start your day with a feeling of joy! It has been medically proven that a positive attitude improves your overall health and well-being. These positive attitudes will bring the other benefits you want. I pray this story will open your mind and help you to see all the Lord's blessings surrounding you at this very moment. Whether it's the purr of a happy kitten, or an unexpected hug, be grateful! There will be far more, who will not even have this small blessing, to help them move forward today.

If you have not asked God to open your eyes to see all the good He has done for you, don't waste another minute! Go ahead and ask Him to open your eyes to see, smell, touch, taste, and feel all the goodness He has offered. There is no greater blessing than to feel His love and presence at work in your life.

Please don't spend so much energy looking for that one significant promise, while missing all the beautiful blessings, as I did! I promise...if you begin to look at life with a new spirit of thankfulness, your wait will be much less anxious. Don't let the blessing of the moment slip by you unnoticed; for it will not be pleasing to the Lord. **1st Timothy 6:6, it says "But godliness with contentment is great gain."**

I pray this helps you experience great joy to do His will, while waiting for His promise. Without a doubt ...it **WILL** *come! He is never too late and He knows us better than we know ourselves. Jesus knows EXACTLY what we need and He never fails! Give God all your thanks; give Him the glory, honor, and praise. Then watch, as He multiplies His blessings back to you. Learn to smell and see the beauty of the rose instead of concentrating on the prick of the thorns. The sweetness of its fragrance will utterly astound you!*

Could I Believe For Everyone Else, YET Not Myself?!
~~~~~~~~~~~~~~~~~~~~~~~~~~~~~~~~~~~~

   I have written many stories, about healing and miracles for others. Yet, as ridiculous as it sounds, I have personally struggled receiving a physical healing for myself. Why? On a daily basis, I see the mistakes I make. Like a neon sign, flashing along the highway in the dark of night, my faults and failures continually parade through my mind, to justify how unworthy I am of His love and grace. I know everyone reading these words make the same mistakes as I do; yet you have most likely experienced the miraculous power of God over and over again working in your life. It seems easier for me to pray and expect an answer for someone else. Why? Because I don't see all of their flaws, or the mistakes they make in their lives.

   Now don't get me wrong, Jesus does not withhold healing just because we are not perfect; I have seen it and been on the receiving end many times. The Bible says, when we ask forgiveness, He casts our mistakes as far as the east is from the west, never to be remembered again. No wonder! The Creator of the universe understood better than anyone, the directions of east and west go on for infinity! It is such a comfort to know our sins are cast away forever! On the other hand, I am human flesh. Therefore, the enemy's "neon sign" flashes on with its constant taunting whisper, that I must try to "EARN" His grace before I "deserve" any of His blessings. Satan's lies urge me to "qualify myself," before God can use me for His Glory. I believe that is why we have trouble stepping out in that realm of faith.

94

Think about it. Scripture reveals Jesus knows us better than we know ourselves. From the inside out, nothing is hidden from His eyes. But, He loves us anyway and His mercy towards us is everlasting. It gives all of us reason to rejoice! I don't know about you, but it makes me want to give Him my very best. I would much rather try and fail, than not try at all.

This point brings us back to square one. I am not hindered praying for the needs of others because I don't see my hands; Jesus is the one touching them through my hands! However, when I pray for myself, the neon lights of self-doubt flash again, and all I can see are my own faults. One of the most disparaging moments of my life allowed Jesus to gain my attention and teach me a valuable lesson.

A few years back, I had both of my main tendons snap at the same time in my right arm! I later found out it was caused by some earlier medications I had been prescribed. It was Christmas Eve, and I was on my way to the family gathering, at my sister and brother-in-loves home, where about forty -eight of us gather together and exchange presents. I had to grab a few Christmas gift bags, so I stopped at the local Dollar Tree store.

I approached the front door of the store, and was about half way inside, when suddenly an elderly woman, with her hands full of packages, charged through the half opened door heading out from the inside. I am sure she assumed I was strong enough to hold the door for her, but rushing me like she did, left me no room to hold it properly! Since I was NOT the type to let the door slam into her, I tried my best to hold it. Reaching backwards, holding it as best as I could with just my fingertips, I felt my arm snap so hard I heard the sound!

As she turned to glance at me, the expression on her face said she heard it, too!

The pain I felt was horrific! I went to the planned dinner trying my best to appear normal, but every movement of my arm caused such pain, it forced me to suck my breath in from total agony.

Later that night, I was in for a rude awakening. I thought a good night's rest would make things better in the morning. Using pillows, I had to prop my arm in a perfectly level position to even think about falling asleep. As I drifted off in total exhaustion, the slightest movement awakened me and caused me to cry out in pain. Keeping Glenn awake made me feel even worse. Each time my arm would drop downward, the tendon would rip through more tissue causing horrific pain, as it curled up more inside the muscle. Of course, this pain was not gone in the morning at all; it went on for literal months!

I had terrible insurance. Very few specialists would even consider taking it. Still, I finally had to look for a doctor, who would at least look at the problem. I had to get this fixed! I could not deal with the pain anymore. I finally found a downstate doctor's office that accepted my insurance and made an appointment. I was thankful they scheduled it quickly: I only had to wait a couple of days. As this doctor examined me, he asked, "Can you move the arm like this?" He tried many different positions, but I could not comply. Finally, he recommended me to try physical therapy. I questioned this, because I had never heard of anyone recommending physical therapy, as a remedy for torn tendons. He very gruffly replied, "Let's get something straight! I have no intention of hunting for rolled up tendons with this insurance. The best I will do is surgically repair the rotator cuff tear, and that's it!"

I was so shocked by the rudely barked reply; I didn't know what to think! However, I made up my mind this doctor would NOT make me cry! It made me feel terrible... as if I was less of a person, because of the type of insurance I had. I would have fared out much better if I had qualified for Medicaid. However, at the time we were a few dollars over the limit, so it was not an option. As he exited the examining room door, he very gruffly instructed me to set my own appointment with the secretary for the therapy, then shut the door promptly behind him.

Now, I was completely crushed, but I still refused to cry! I pulled myself together, and approached the front desk. I spoke to the secretary and let her know I would not need a return appointment, nor would my insurance cover the physical therapy. I continued to hold myself together until we reached our vehicle, and THEN I fell apart, hoping the tears would wash away the terrible ache the doctor had placed in my heart! I could not believe this Physician had spoken to me in such a manner! I cried my heart out, for I knew my relentless suffering was not going to end any time soon. I was at my limits with this pain. Glenn was so beside himself; he could not bear to see me so upset. While trying to drive us home safely, He did his best to try to comfort me.

In the midst of my tears, I cried out loud, "JESUS, did you hear that doctor?" Immediately, the Lord spoke back to me, "You quit crying; I'm going to take care of it!" I stopped crying and related to Glenn what God had just dropped into my heart. He asked if the Lord revealed "how" He was going to take care of it. I replied, "No,

only that He said He would take care of it." It comforted
me so much; I did not shed one more tear. I knew
without a doubt, it was His sweet voice. He had spoken
to me! Feeling much better, we continued our journey
home. Even though the rest of the day, any movement
caused me to endure the same pain I had experienced for
months, I did not wonder WHEN He would fix it or
HOW He would fix it. I only knew He WOULD!

That night as usual, I positioned my arm as
comfortable as possible on the pillows, and quickly
drifted off to sleep. I awoke the next morning shocked! I
realized I had slept the night through. The pain in my
arm never woke me up one time! I went about the early
part of the day as usual, without experiencing ANY pain.
I decided to venture further. I recalled the range of
motion positions the doctor requested in his office the
day prior. I was ecstatic! I could do them all! I was so
thrilled with my healing, I cried from the relief.
Sometime between falling asleep and waking up, the
Great Physician, Jesus Christ, healed my arm. I have
used stretch bands to strengthen the atrophy that took
place, during the months of immobility. You can still see
the bulge where the tendons are curled up in my arm
muscle; but to me, it is simply a constant visible
reminder of the miracle Jesus performed in my life.

That night, God showed me He truly does care.
Oh, by the way, those neon flashing signs now say, "He
will heal me, too!" It was so silly of me to think
otherwise. In prayer, I thank him for His love and
kindness each day. There is no greater friend to have
than Jesus. Proverbs: 18:24 says, "There is a friend that
sticketh closer than a brother." He didn't have to heal
me... I surely didn't earn it. It makes me desire to love

and serve Him even more! I could never repay all of His goodness to me. This wonderful miracle happened several years ago. Although I am unable to lift heavy objects, I still use that arm every day...PAIN FREE!

I hope sharing these stories, helps someone else to believe. Jesus loved you before you even knew who He was. He is the One that breathed life into your body the moment you were born. Jesus is waiting for you to call on Him. GO NOW! Tell Him, you want to develop a deeper relationship and that you want to know Him more! He will touch your heart like He did mine. That's just how good my Jesus is!

Pat Gilliss   The Other Side of Broken

Church Prayers
Heard and Answered
~~~~~~

A few years ago; Hurricane Sandy swept along the outer edges of Delaware. Although there was significant beach erosion, I don't recall any homes being destroyed or any loss of life; we were very blessed. However, the Atlantic City coastal region of New Jersey was ravaged very hard by the brunt of the storm.

Our son, Wayne Gilliss, Pastor of Life Point church in Pleasantville, lived only minutes away from the Atlantic City shoreline. As his mother, I was very concerned about their welfare and I called him to make sure they were all safe. Although they personally survived without any damage, it was overwhelming to hear the stress in his voice, as he described the desolate condition of so many others in their community. He told me that their home was only five minutes from that horrific destruction.

As a pastor, it was tough for him and his precious wife, Paula, to witness some of their own church family's suffering such terrible losses. There was one unfortunate woman, whose rental home floated out to sea with all her belongings inside. So many lost so much, while others lost all! To say this was a bad storm, would be an enormous understatement... it was a catastrophe! For days, photos published by the news media testified of the massive flooding and destruction.

The church members, who were not affected by the storm, responded immediately to the Pastor's plea for donations and supplies, to help those in need. They were not just concerned for their parish; their hearts

100

were broken for the entire surrounding community. The congregation's donations were overwhelming; these precious people gave more than Wayne and Paula could have even imagined. There was no doubt they gave until it hurt!

Wayne said, "I knew they were a tremendous group of people, but it was so beautiful to see such a display of love and compassion during this tragic time." The huge fellowship hall was overflowing with boxes. Canned good, meats, fruits, vegetables, and cases of water filled the tables. Boxes of cleaning supplies, over the counter medications, hygiene supplies, disposable diapers, blankets, and wipes were packed for quick distribution. Anything they thought could be useful, including a mountain of nice clothing and good shoes were brought to the church.

Wayne notified the local Police Department and the Red Cross, that supplies would be available and forwarded the church address. Word spread quickly. The following morning, as they opened their doors, the line of people seemed endless. By nightfall, several hundred people had been helped. I may be off a bit in this count, but not by far. However, with the exception of a few remaining clothing items, their supplies were depleted in one day!

Wayne and Paula, asked the people of the Church to help them pray and ask God what to do. He knew his church members had already given sacrificially, and there was no way, just one day later, they could afford to give a second time.

That night, he went home trying to be happy they helped as many as they did. Yet, knowing tomorrow they had nothing more to hand out, but some clothing and a few pairs of shoes, pained his heart.

The following morning, while Wayne was sorting through the remaining clothing, a tractor trailer pulled into the church parking lot. The truck driver walked in and asked, "Who is going to unload this truck?" Pastor Gilliss asked the man, "What is on the truck to unload?" The driver explained, "The Police Department, and the Red Cross, told us your church is handing out supplies, to the storm victims." Pastor Gilliss replied, "It is, but we ran out in one day!" The guy driving the truck said, "Well, I brought you a truck full of supplies, all the way from OHIO!" What a miracle! The Pastor had seen God answer prayers many times before; yet, it was so thrilling to see such an enormous blessing and answer to prayer come so quickly! **It was one of those prayers Isaiah 65:24 says, "And it shall come to pass, that before they call, I will answer; and while they yet speak I will hear."**

God was right on time; they were able to continue blessing others. Day after day, they all worked very hard from morning till night. The lines formed for weeks, and miraculously the supply trucks kept coming. God's supplies never ran dry. Donations poured in from everywhere. In fact, it reached a point they needed three warehouses for storage and the owners of those facilities donated the space free of charge! Were the blessings "...pressed down, shaken together, and running over..." You better believe they were! That is the God we serve!

In addition to being Pastor, our son holds a regular job as well. However, he was able to switch his hours around in order to be at the church as much as possible. There were times; he was the only one available to unload the trucks. Other places of employment did not allow that flexibility for the men of his congregation; still each day, they came when they could. As his parent's, he related to us the many times a day he prayed, "God, if you will give me the strength to do this, I will." Somehow, it came. He said, "Mom, at times I didn't think we could make our legs make one more trip across that floor, but God strengthened us all to keep moving." This wonderful group of people stood strongly behind their Pastor and his wife; diligently they worked whatever hours they could, until the emergency was over. Every aspect of their prayers was answered, for God not only provided the necessities, He blessed them with daily strength to see the task through. It was amazing and our hearts overflowed to see their love and respect for not only the ministry, but towards their fellow man, who were complete strangers to them, but not to a God, who loves everyone.

As the immediate needs were met each day, the lines began to diminish. Because their homes and belongings were destroyed, many were waiting for insurance settlements and survived for weeks living in their vehicles. Pastor Gilliss made each individual family know the warehouses were still full of bedding, dishes, silverware, pots, pans, lamps, generators, kerosene heaters, and almost everything that was necessary, to start over again. When they found a place to live, they were to return and choose whatever they desired. For several months, one by one, that is exactly what they did. True to his word, they obtained most of what they needed to set up housekeeping again. It was such a blessing to hear the thankfulness in their voices and see the tears of joy on each face. When weeks passed, with no one coming to get help, they assumed all

*the needs had been met. The blessings continued, as all
the remaining items were distributed to several other
local charity organizations.*

*In the very beginning, as the Pastor began unloading
the very first truck, news media from Ohio appeared
with their cameras. Apparently, they decided to tag
along and follow the story. The photos of devastation and
long lines would allow the generous donors to see their
relief efforts in action. However, Wayne was never one
for the limelight. As he continued his work, his answers
were brief and to the point; he certainly didn't want
publicity for doing something he was happy to do. In
fact, he does not even know I have written this story! I
will surprise them all. I know he would continue to say,
"It wasn't a big deal!" Jesus said if we so much as hand
a cup of water to someone else in His name, it would be
as if we had handed it to Him, and He would bless it.
Wayne, Paula, their children, and congregation,
displayed the wonderful love of Christ in this situation
for months!*

*As his mom, I wanted to give God the glory and
share this beautiful story with the world. Glenn and I
are so proud of our son, daughter- in- love,
grandchildren, and the congregation of Life Point
Church. It took them all to help make this particular
miracle happen! Compassion, kindness, and unending
agape love, reached multitudes and added rays of "SON"
shine in the darkest days of their lives. When you are in
your storms of life, and you have done all you can do, go
to JESUS! He loves you and He is never too busy to hear
your heart's cry. He IS the answer, and He will hear
your prayers. While you may not get everything exactly
as you asked for it, I can assure you; He will send you*

everything you need.

Sometimes, it may be grapes and a quiet breeze, and sometimes He may put a shovel in your hands, like in this case. But, it's always what the Master knows is best for His children. Whatever He sends your way will help you move the mountain that stands before you. Just trust Him. He will see you through. I have proved Him many times over, and He's never failed me yet. He awaits your call, and is longing to lead you to a better life. He already knows your name.

But For the Grace of God,
My Complete Testimony

~~~~~~

Note: The story you are about to read is true. These narratives were shared to bring hope to those, who in childhood had no control over the circumstances life afforded them. No matter what you have been through or where you are today...there is HOPE! Regardless of your background, Jesus loves "YOU"! If you will give your life to Him, He has the power to pull you out of the clutches of the past and lead you into a future far greater than anything you could have possibly imagined.

I have simply skimmed the surface of the hardships I faced as a child. Please, understand I am not seeking your sympathy. I am delighted with my life. God has opened the Heavens, and poured so many blessings on my beautiful family, you would be wasting your efforts. What God has healed, IS HEALED, and covered by His blood forever! All I want from this is to help you understand, there is a better life awaiting you. I am anticipating response from many, whose lives will be forever changed. Let your confidence and strength be renewed; Hebrews 12:2 says... "The Author and Finisher of our faith..." is waiting, with pen in hand, to write the rest of your life's story!

Most of these memories occurred before our family began serving the Lord. Once Christ came into our hearts, He miraculously healed broken relationships and completely turned our family dynamics around! We became a loving, forgiving, very closely knit, family. He replaced the turmoil with peace, turned hatred into love, and "existing" into genuinely "living", for the first time in our lives.

Holidays, especially Thanksgiving, normally escalated into an after dinner family feud, with someone storming out the door in anger. For more than forty years now, after dinner , sit around the table or gather in the living room singing songs of praise and giving thanks to God, for all the blessings He has given us throughout the year. From the youngest child to the oldest adult, we share testimonies of answered prayers and express our love to each other. Instead of criticism, jealousy, anger, and resentment, we provide each other with strength, encouragement, and a shoulder to lean on. We pray together and share one another's burdens. The joy we experience is more precious than gold! Had we not turned to the Lord, this transformation would have never taken place! If God did this for our family, He can and will do it for yours. It will take time, but don't lose faith. You will eventually begin to see changes occur one small thing at a time.

*This beautiful new life was made possible, because of a very young couple. Pastor Royce Andrus, and his precious wife, Glenda, gave up their personal desires and followed the calling of God, to a mission field on the east coast. They somehow knew our dysfunctional family was part of His plan and saw us through His eyes. They literally spoke **words of life** into us. When the only thing someone chooses to see in you is the good, wonderful things begin to happen! In fact, the Thanksgiving tradition we have now practiced for many years, began with them. Unselfishly, they continually poured agape love on us, and in just a short time, over forty members of our family were filled with the Holy Spirit! To date, not counting throngs of others, they* *have affected five generations of our family alone. That is what a real burden for the lost will do.*

If God did this for my family, He can surely change your situation, too! It depends entirely on your circumstances. If He sees best to "mend fences".... He will. However, if He knows it's best to repair your life in another way, keep trusting; ask His guidance knowing, as long as you stay in tune with Him, He will guide your every step.

Please allow me to share the story of my life. I will not say writing my testimony will be easy, but I have asked for His help to write this with all the grace and humility I can. Now...on with the story.

Growing up, my life was very challenging. Being the oldest girl placed a huge responsibility on two very young shoulders. Actually, I should say on two sets of shoulders, for my sister, JoAnn and I were born only eleven months apart. In my first book, "You Asked God for WHAT?!", I mentioned there were six children, but the two of us were given the responsibility of running the entire household. At ages seven and eight, JoAnn and I cared for Karen, our one year old baby sister, along with our two younger brothers, Ronnie and Neil. Since he was the oldest, our nine year old brother, Jack, thought he was the boss of everyone. On occasion, if the notion struck him, he helped. But like any other nine year old boy, he seized every opportunity to play ball with his friends.

We prepared a breakfast of toast and coffee, then packed lunches, which by Thursday, consisted of butter, or ketchup sandwiches. The peanut butter and jelly were usually gone by then. In the evening, JoAnn peeled the potatoes and put the vegetables in the pans to cook. I stood on a chair to light the gas burner and fry the meat, watching to make sure nothing burned. With the exception of Karen, the baby, we all helped with the dishes.

Mom and Dad both worked outside of the home. Daddy worked three jobs. Mom was an excellent typist and worked for the Vibert Company addressing envelopes for two cents each. After the typing position ended, she worked at E. J. Korvettes in Trenton, New Jersey, as a sales clerk. This job kept her from home many nights and weekends.

While we did see Mom most nights, our Daddy came home from his full time construction job, ate dinner, and left immediately for his second full time job, cleaning airplanes on the base at Fort Dix, in New Jersey. Eventually, lack of sleep and exhaustion became quite an issue. He found a better position just a few blocks from home, at Carslake Community Center in Bordentown. He cleaned the building every evening and spent Saturday mornings cutting their grass. Saturday evenings and Sunday mornings, he cleaned the local Presbyterian church. He did not actually receive money for this, but his hours were traded toward payment of our monthly rent.

I am sure you can imagine our very unhappy hearts, as most of our time we were home alone. Can you imagine six small children, including an infant, trying to do everything they were supposed to do, and not get into trouble? Most of the time was spent fighting and arguing among ourselves. I remember dreading the winter the most; the five o'clock darkness brought many lonely hours and a sense of fear much worse than the cold howling winds outside.

I was young; I am not sure if Dad still held his second job. Mom babysat during the days now. Yet, somehow they managed to join three separate leagues and went bowling three times a week. To make it worse, they bowled on the late leagues and usually were not home until eleven o'clock at night. I don't think they realized how much we dreaded being left alone, or how badly it frightened us. I am certain it was an extremely hard time for them. Raising six small children in a house that was way too small, and the mounting bills attached to it, could not have been easy. To them, it was simply a brief escape from the pressure.

We loved both of our parents, but I must add...in our hearts, there were times of great anger. For instance, we didn't go to school looking nearly our best. Our ragged and dirty clothes made us a huge target for ridicule, and we were bullied by our peers. Needless to say, "friends" were very few, and there were not many we could count on. So my memories of those times, except for Christmas, are not great ones. Perhaps that is why, to this day, Christmas remains my very favorite time of year. Whenever I even start feeling depressed, I think of Christmas time, either past or approaching, and it lifts my spirits. If I get sad, I play Christmas music no matter what time of year it is. I will share with you only a couple of incidents, embedded in my mind that I have never been able to forget. As you will read, one wonderful teacher gave me hope for the future, the other chose to leave gaping wounds in my tender heart, which bled over into my adulthood...until Jesus stepped in and helped me overcome by the power of His blood!

I treasure the memories of my second grade teacher Mrs. McGowan was so sweet to me. Her love and influence was comparable to the story I wrote about my Aunt Marie, in my second book, "No More Crumbs." She never seemed to notice my ripped and dirty clothing, or my poorly combed hair. It was relatively long and very hard for a seven year old to manage. Mrs. McGowan noticed "me" for who I was, and searched for the gifts within me. She was the sweetest lady in my life at this time.

One thing she did notice was, that at seven years old, I could sing. She loved to hear me. At music time, she would stand me up in front of the entire class and ask me to sing. While it would embarrass me, it also made me feel good because someone truly liked something about me. She also secured a place for me to sing in the school play at Christmas that year. Even though no one from my family would be there to hear me, I did my very best. One day, she told me I would grow up to be a great singer! ME? I did not see how that could be possible; yet, something inside my little seven year old heart believed every word she spoke. Not only was it an epic event... up to this point, it was the highlight of my life!

Mrs. McGowan lived a few houses down from the school. One day, this blessed woman took our entire class to her house and treated us to lunch! I must say, this memory is forever etched in my mind. She had the most beautiful, shiny, tile, floors I have ever seen. I remember saying, "I have never seen such beautiful floors in my whole life!" I could not take my eyes off of them; the tiles were like glass. As I stepped on them, I feared at any moment they might break. Walking across the floor, my shoes made a snapping sound. Seeing my reaction, she gently said, "When you grow up, Patty, you

can have shiny floors just like these." I was shocked at
the thought "I" could live in such a place, but I embraced
her every word. I am now sixty- six years old and, to this
day, my hardwood floors and tiles are kept shiny!

Even before I knew Him, God had His hand on my
life. Using those words, spoken to me as a child, He
began orchestrating my steps toward the future. I began
singing with my sisters, JoAnn and Karen. We had a
very tight family harmony. People seemed to enjoy
hearing us; however, we knew it was the presence of the
Lord we were singing about, that touched their hearts
the most. Without Him, it would have been nothing! Our
Pastor often asked us to minister in song, and we were
honored. Eventually, we formed the Murray Trio and
began singing in our tristate area. Miraculously, God
opened the door for us to make a recording! Oh, the
power of words spoken into a child's life.

Several years later, I was surprised to find Mrs.
McGowan's son was now operating the Men's clothing
store they still owned on the main street of Bordentown,
when I was just a little girl. After relating my story, he
gladly gave me her address. I wrote to her, telling of the
influence she had in my life and the loving memories I
held in my heart. I wanted her to know I had not
forgotten her love towards me. The time she invested
was not in vain. I enclosed a copy of the recording. Her
son told me that she listened to it every day.

Being in her class was like Heaven to me. As I
write this story, sweet feelings for this angelic woman
warm my heart. My heartfelt prayer is, "Dear Jesus, I
hope I can impact someone's life like she impacted
mine!" Knowing I was leaving her class to enter third
grade was very hard on me. I was mournful and suffered

what they now call "separation anxiety". I did not want to move away from the love I felt in her classroom. Very calmly, Mrs. McGowan assured me I would love third grade just as well. I trusted she was right.

Regretfully, my third grade teacher was not nearly as kind to me. She appeared to care only about the wealthy children. In retrospect, they were all so clean and well dressed, my small naive mind may have "surmised" their families were well off, whether they were or not. Regardless, in this new classroom, the teacher seemed to find pleasure by embarrassing me. While I vividly remember many things, there are four situations that stand out in my mind.

One day, she called me to her side at the front of the classroom. I had no idea what she was about to say. The children were questioned, "Does anyone have any hand-me-downs you can give to Patty, so she can come to school dressed nicely?" I remember one girl, whose father owned a car dealership, swiftly raising her hand saying, "I think I can!" In reflection, I realize she felt pretty badly for me and it was truly a sweet gesture. However, at that moment, I wanted the floor to open up and swallow me, so I would never be seen or heard from again. I was quite mature for a third grader; I knew what it felt like to be embarrassed many times. However, what happened next took it to a whole new level. The following Monday, the girl brought a bag of clothing for all the children to see. As the girl handed it to me, my face burned like fire! I accepted it with a smile, and a thank you, knowing if I didn't, facing the teacher's wrath for my ungratefulness would be much worse. I was so humiliated; I thought I would die before school was over for that day!

Arriving home, I quickly hid the bag containing the dress and matching socks, before Mom came home from work. In my heart, I really loved them and could not convince myself to throw them away. What if the teacher asked me if I still had them? I could not lie to her; however, I did not want to embarrass my Mom either. Somehow bringing the bag into the house, made me feel as though I had done something wrong. I was merely eight at the time, so I hid them. I can remember laying on the bed, and falling asleep thinking, "What if Mom finds them?"

One day, a few weeks later, she was searching for something and discovered the hidden bag of clothing. She questioned me and wanted to know where they came from. I HAD to tell her the truth. Angrily, she threw them away saying, " You tell her you will NEVER wear them!" She was very hurt and felt embarrassed herself. Once again, it was my fault; I felt so sorry I had hurt her! It was a very heavy load for an eight year old to carry in her heart.

Weeks went by before the dreaded moment came. In front of the entire class, the teacher asked, "Why won't you wear the lovely outfit you received from K?" I boldly answered, "My Mom said I will NEVER wear them!" Immediately, things became worse than ever!

As the Christmas season drew near, our school principal, Miss Anna T. Burr made an announcement. "Shoe Boots" had just hit the market, and were at the top of most Christmas lists that year. In fact, we were all hoping to have a pair under our tree. However, Miss Burr had decided the black rubber soles would leave marks on the hallway floors, and announced they could not be worn to school. I was very disappointed to hear this news.

Sure enough, each of us received a pair of those wonderful shoe boots! I loved them and was heartbroken to tell Daddy about the announcement. Sadly, I said, "Daddy, if we wear these boots to school, we will get into trouble! No one is allowed to wear them!" As he spoke, the look on his face was as firm as the sound of his voice, "Well, you tell Miss Burr if she wants you to wear something different, she can just buy them herself!"

Can you imagine what the balance of my Christmas vacation was like? Knowing on my return, I had to face Miss Anna T. Burr? She was tall and slender, and wore old fashion, black laced shoes, that were fat heeled and about two inches high. As she walked the corridors, they clipped loudly on the shiny tile floors. Her very short silvery white hair and pursed lips made her demeanor appear even worse. She had a terrible temper! Secretly, the students gave her the name "Two Gun Annie"! I do not know what he did, but one day, a young boy got into trouble. I witnessed her temper in full mode, as she grabbed him by the upper arm and kicked him in the seat of his britches with the side of her foot, all the way to the office! Her face was so beet red, I thought for sure it would explode. Now, I had to go tell her what my Daddy said! I fell asleep each night, imagining what she would do to me. I dreaded facing her!

Vacation was over. The day had arrived, and my little heart was terrified of walking into my classroom. I knew without a doubt, as soon as Miss Teacher saw my shoe boots; she was going to make an example of me. She spotted them almost immediately. "Patty Murray, what do you think you are doing wearing those shoe boots to school? Did you hear Miss Burr's announcement before

*Christmas break?" Sheepishly, I replied, "Yes, Ma'am.
She questioned further, "Then WHY are you wearing
them?" As bold as an eight year old could muster, I
replied, "My daddy said... if Miss Burr doesn't like them
she can buy me something better herself!" With a face
redder than her smeared red lipstick, I was instructed
to, "just march my sassy self-right down to the
Principal's office and tell her what my Daddy said!" The
thought I might be facing serious trouble with the
Principal seemed to give her pleasure. In retrospect, I
will never understand why she asked me the question
and became angry, because I answered it truthfully.*

*Outside the classroom door, the Principal's office
was at the opposite end of an extremely long hallway. It
was the longest walk of my life. I am not sure which side
of the family it came from; but rehearsing what I should
say in my mind, brought my little Irish / Indian boldness
to the surface. Bracing myself, I walked into the office.
The counter was so high, I did not see anyone. However,
Mrs. Blanch, the secretary peered over the top and said,
"Well, little Miss Murray, what can I do for you?" I
replied, "Miss Teacher told me to come tell Miss Burr
what my Daddy said!"*

*There was no time to think further. Miss Burr
had heard me; immediately, in her gruff no nonsense
voice said, "Well, what did your Daddy say?" I thought I
would speak the words, and then die on the spot! Taking
a deep breath, just in case it WOULD be my last, I
stomped my foot and said, "My Daddy said if you don't
like my shoe boots, YOU can buy me better ones
yourself!" I felt like Shirley Temple in the movie, "The
Little Princess," facing the stern girls school matron. I
expected her to come over that counter top toward me,*

*like a fire breathing dragon! Spankings were allowed at
that time, and I fully believed in a moment, I would be a
recipient. Instead, Miss Burr was so surprised, she burst
into uncontrollable laughter! I was in shock, and could
hardly believe my eyes. Finally, pulling herself together,
she said, "Well, you tell Miss Teacher "I" said, we will
make an exception for you Murray children. You can go
on back to your class." She was still laughing to herself,
as she walked away from the counter, and out of my
sight!*

*Well, that went much better than I expected, until
suddenly, I remembered who I was going to face next!
The walk back to the classroom seemed much longer
than the one to the Principal's office. I knew facing her
would be very hard; the news would not be taken very
well. She was visibly angry the exception was made for
our family, and things only became worse for me in that
class.*

*Another incident I vividly recall was Math class in
Miss Teacher's room; it was just prior to lunch. Column
addition was very hard for me. I hated adding all those
numbers! She encouraged us by announcing, "Children,
if you get all the problems correct, you may go out to the
playground until lunchtime." Even if she found some
mistakes, we were allowed to rework them, until they
were correct, and join the others outside.*

*This news was inspiring! I struggled so hard, day
after day, but I just couldn't master the long columns of
numbers. A kind boy, named Gary, sat in front of me.
One day, he said, "Patty, if you take your time, you will
get them all right. Don't rush!" I did just what he
suggested; instead of hurrying, I took my time.*

Miss Teacher looked over my completed paper for

117

what seemed like eternity! Finally, with her red pen, she placed a huge "C" for "correct" at the top of the page. It was on my very first attempt, and I can still remember the happiness that filled my heart! The victory was short lived, for her next words were, "I can't believe you got them all correct. Did you look at someone else's paper?" I quickly replied, "NO, I did NOT!" My feelings were crushed; I had never cheated and it pained my heart she even thought I would! Continuing to scan my paper, she said "Oh, look here. You forgot to dot one of the "i's" in the name Patricia. Anyone who can't spell their own name correctly doesn't deserve to go outside, take your seat!" Returning to my chair I thought, even if the others had some errors, they were allowed to make the corrections. If it was only for five minutes, like the others, I would have been given permission to go to the playground. Yet, because I missed dotting an "i" in my name, I had to remain at my desk.

My spirit was not only crushed that day, it was broken. Looking back, this was the defining moment I realized "winning" was not for me. No matter how hard I tried, I would never be good enough! For the rest of that very long school year, during math class, not once did I join the other children outside. I simply gave up trying. Every day, during Math class, I remembered her words, and it felt as though it had just happened.

In reflection, I now understand why I never trusted another teacher. My little heart was set in stone that day, and I knew there was no sense in trying anymore. Until I left high school, I made it through each class by the skin of my teeth. Miss Teacher broke my spirit, and it just would not heal.

Miss Teacher's final blow took its toll on my

already weak self-esteem. It was early spring; I was on the playground during lunch recess. I loved the swings, but it had rained the night before and as usual, a huge puddle formed on the ground directly under the seat. Normally, I pulled the swing sideways and held both chains tightly in my hands. Making one huge hop, I jumped safely on the seat before it reached the waterhole. Not today...I missed the seat and landed in the cold dirty water with a thud! I was soaking wet and covered with mud. My shoes squished and squeaked loudly, as I walked across the main school yard. They probably heard me coming a half mile away!

As upset as I was from the fall, it was what I was about to face that frightened me more. Miss Teacher loved to seize every opportunity she could to embarrass me. Today was no exception. She immediately marched me to the school nurse's office, and asked if she had a clean outfit I could wear for the rest of the day. The nurse assured her she would find something suitable.

They held a conversation, as if I was not even standing there! Miss Teacher began, "She really needs a ROYAL scrubbing... from her hair down." It made me feel terrible to hear them say such unkind things about my Mom and Dad. I wanted to scream, "Stop!" But, instead I said nothing; I was already in enough trouble. Suddenly, I heard my teacher ask, "Is there any way you can take her to the gym shower and do that?" I began crying loudly; I kept saying, "NO!" I had never been in a shower before; they were relatively new and mostly only wealthy people had them installed. It sounded very frightening to me. My screaming and cries of, "PLEASE, STOP!" fell on deaf ears, as she practically dragged me into that monster size shower room.

I vividly recall someone walking into the room to see what all the commotion was about. As I looked up, there stood the school janitor! He was staring at me! I was nearly nine years old, and it was the WORST personal moment I had EVER experienced. To say I was embarrassed, humiliated and scared, would be an understatement!

This one incident was so traumatizing, I will never be able to forget it. I told no one, especially not my parents, until one day at the age of sixty- four, I was finally able to share the horrible memory with my husband, Glenn. I truly believe that my third grade school year stripped every fiber of my self-esteem. While reading this story repeatedly to make corrections, I realized just how much this third grade school year made me feel like I could never become anything significant in life. While it laid dormant in the eves of my mind and heart...it continued to hold me captive. Once I finally dealt with it, I believe I can achieve anything I set my mind to. Once again, my dreams and aspirations are alive and I AM successful!

If you are an Elementary, Sunday School, or Daycare teacher, please remember some children have unwanted responsibilities placed on their small shoulders, and are not capable of performing tasks their parents should be held accountable to do! If God has entrusted you with students living in these circumstances, for their benefit, let disdain be replaced with a spirit of love and compassion! Children comprehend more than you think. Quietly comparing themselves to their classmates, they already see the difference! One more negative stroke could affect their lives forever. If anything, give more love; for you do not know what they may have endured their last few hours at home. Every compliment will lift self-esteem. Be the wind beneath their wings and teach them they can fly above any circumstance!

Parents, God has given you precious gifts! If you know you are lacking, pray and ask Him to help you improve your parenting skills and give you direction. Lift your child's self-esteem and make sure they start their day looking and feeling their very best. Make your home a "haven"; create a loving environment, watered with love and kind spoken words! Stand behind them, pray before they go out the door, and send them to school knowing you believe in them. It truly makes all the difference in the world.

Time marched on; as a teenager, I became very sad. I was overtaken by depression. My home was not the "happy place" I described above. I completed eighth grade and moved on to high school with very few treasured moments, however, nothing remotely compared to my third grade experience. That trauma alone was enough to last a lifetime!

Please keep in mind; we were not a Christian family during this time. Daddy was a "man's man"...he had been raised to believe, even if a woman had a full time job, it was still her sole responsibility to handle all of the house work, laundry, and children. I can recall him saying, "Cooking is woman's work!" In reflection, he worked three jobs. Even if his feelings were different, there would have been no time for him to help my Mother.

At the age of fourteen, we moved back to Delaware. I guess by this time, my heart was hardened to the point I simply ignored most things. I suffered untold bullying, and pretty much became a loner. By now, life had scarred me well. At a very early age, I became tough! I learned to trust NO ONE; therefore, they would not have the power to hurt me. If someone hit me, I hit them back... harder...both physically and verbally! In my childhood, my parents were unaware of many other things that happened to me. Even now, I dare not utter them. At age fifteen, my only goal was to reach age sixteen, so I could quit school in the tenth grade...and I did!

Now I had to find a job. My Dad was pleased he would have a little extra money. He took every dime I earned! All of a sudden, my "job" became my "prison." During his younger life, that is how it was done. He simply carried the "learned behavior" forward. Pent up anger was a kind description for what I was honestly feeling. I saw no way out and had no future goals; handing over my hard earned paycheck was it. I dared not argue the matter. This continued over a year. At least, my Dad seemed to love me now. Whenever Mom began her railings about what I didn't do right, he stood up for me.

I finally found the nerve and asked to keep at least seven dollars a week out of my pay. After lengthy consideration, he agreed. I found a Chevy Impala convertible for one hundred and sixty dollars! I loved it! But out of the seven dollars, I was responsible for purchasing clothes, gas, and personal needs. In addition, I had to save enough to repay him ten dollars a month, until my car was paid off. To accomplish this, I collected gas money from everyone who rode with me. This lifestyle went on for about a year; it was like Heaven to me! My eighteenth birthday was fast approaching and I counted the days until I would be free!

An Aunt, whom I dearly loved, invited me to live with her in New Jersey. She offered to help me find a job; all she expected of me was ten dollars a week room and board. This was the most exciting news I had heard in quite a while! As soon as I became of age, I announced my plans to my parents. I was moving out and was going to live with Aunt Lucy and Uncle Wes. Dad was devastated; he promised if I remained at home, room and board would only be twenty- five dollars a week. Keep in mind, at the time, minimum wage was only one dollar and forty- three cents an hour. I was employed at a poultry processing plant. I put in over forty hours of back breaking work each week, and this was still a considerable amount to hand over to my parents! In order to have enough money for myself, I would still have to secure another, part time job.

It was during this time in my life, I met my first husband; the biological father of my two oldest children. I did not realize it would end up becoming another extremely abusive relationship. Oh, the pain I endured! All of a sudden, I found myself out of the frying pan and into the fire! As a defense mechanism, I hardened my heart even more. Without a doubt, I could curse any sailor under the table. If you did not like me, you had the rest of your life to get over it! I couldn't care less! I was well trained to defend myself. Anyone, who began yelling loudly in my face, swiftly discovered they were on the wrong end of my anger! I smoked three packs of cigarettes a day. I remember saying to myself, "When cigarettes go to eighty- five cents a pack, I am going to quit smoking." Well, they did. However, quitting was not as easy as I thought it was going to be. With the exception of my two treasures, Amy and Wayne, my life was miserable! I remember my sister, JoAnn, saying to me, "Patty, if you come to my church, Jesus will help you quit smoking! "Really?" Eventually, I thought it was worth a try. My Mom and Dad began going with her, and the change in their lives was outstanding; I knew there had to be something to this Jesus thing. It helped me make my decision.

Because our marriage was pretty rocky, we decided our whole family should begin going to church. Many times, the Pastor's wife, Sister Glenda Andrus, greeted me at the door with a heartfelt hug, and say, "You are so precious." What? You must understand, up to this point in my life, "Precious" was never an adjective used to describe ME! So, I certainly did not believe her words. Still, like a healing ointment, they worked their way into my innermost being. Every time she spoke those words of love, a warm glow filled my heart. Instantly, my mind reminisced to Mrs. McGowan. Since second grade, no one had ever treated me so loving and kind ...until now.

Time and time again, she spoke words of love and affirmation to me. Slowly, I found myself subconsciously striving to become the woman she seemed to see in me. I loved the church, after all these heartbreaking years...I loved "feeling loved"! Her words were powerful; she literally spoke words of life into my broken heart and bruised spirit! I continued to grow in the Lord. I made up my mind to go "cold turkey" and lay my cigarette habit aside. It took six months, but JoAnn was right; God helped me!

Not long after, my husband at that time decided this was not the life for us. He decided "WE" would stop *going. I was devastated! I loved God! I loved this church and the members loved me! His narcissist personality demanded full control. He became threatened by the confidence he saw growing in me, and once again, the need to isolate me from others surfaced. After much prayer, I decided he could leave if he wanted to, but the children and I were not going to give up this beautiful new life we had found. I knew God was with me; there was no other way I would have had the strength and courage to tell him, "NO"! The children and I continued to attend services and grow in the Lord. For a while, things seemed to be going fairly well... but it did not last long.*

After twelve long years, I found the courage and strength to leave. The physical and verbal abuse had been relentless, and the numerous instances of infidelity took its toll on my heart. I choose to let the rest remain private. Even if I disclosed the ugly details, I am not sure you could bring yourself to believe them. Do I carry scars from all of it? Yes! But, I serve a powerful God, who has dramatically helped me heal from my pain! I can honestly say I have forgiven EVERYONE, who has hurt me in the past. I am sharing my story to help YOU. Forgiveness is a powerful force! Because Jesus helped me find the strength, I have been SET FREE from so much heartache.

God picked up all the broken and shattered pieces of my life, and placed them back together, as only He could. I met, as I lovingly call him, "My Glenn". He not only loved me, but he adopted my two treasures and loved us with all of his heart. He made an enormous difference in our lives. From the very beginning, I knew he was sent to us by God, Himself! When our twins were

*born, he continued to love and treat them all the same.
My older children adore him to this day and call him
"Dad". We all love him... especially me. He is my real life
hero!*

*We have been married thirty-four years now. At
sixty-six years of age, dreams are still coming to pass!
In the past five years, I have written three books. I
happily reside with my gift from God, "My Glenn". Our
children have all married well, and we have the added
blessing of eleven grandchildren. We owe the Lord so
much for His goodness to us. We may slow down with
age, but plan on reaching for souls until Jesus comes!*

*I want to tell the world how good God is! I am still
working on being more like Him... to love like
He loves. I am not flawless; nor, am I all I want to
become. However, by His grace, I have come a long way
from what I used to be! I have not disclosed all of the
afflictions and trials I have suffered... just enough for
you to get the picture. I wrote these words for someone...
somewhere, who may be at the bottom of life. I want you
to know, YOU can make it! If one person climbs out of
the "crab pot" and escapes the "claws" of the world
desiring to pull you down, as humbling as it is, it will
have been worth bearing my embarrassment and shame,
for all of humanity to read.*

*If you will call on Jesus in prayer, and turn your
life over to Him, He will hear and answer! Everything
will not change overnight, hard times will still exist; but
you will not walk through them alone. God will open
doors you never thought were possible. One day, you will
glance backward and notice the mountain that stood in
front of you for years, now appears to be only an ant hill
on the horizon! There is nothing like the sweet taste of*

victory! It is NEVER too late to start your life over for the better. There is no sin He will not forgive, no pain He cannot touch, and no heart Jesus cannot mend. There is nothing you can say He has not heard before, and you certainly cannot shock Him! Best of all... you cannot out love Him. Please remember... in the long term, suppressing your emotions will only result in more heartache and anguish. Give it all to Jesus and allow Him to help you. He desires to do for you, what he did for me! He loves you dearly and is awaiting your call.

A Little Girl's Crooked Spine Is Straightened

~~~~~~~~~~~~~~~~~~~~~~~~~~~~~~~~~~~~~~

My back condition was growing continually worse. I needed surgery, but I had been without health insurance for ten years and could do nothing about it. Suddenly, God miraculously opened the door; a health provider finally accepted my application and my heart flooded with thankfulness and relief! Yet, in the midst of celebration, a shadow hung over my spirit. The terrible outcomes I had witnessed among my friends, and the horror stories related from others were disturbing. I just wasn't sure I could go through with this surgery.

"Jesus," I asked, "I have been praying for my back for twenty years. I am distraught that I am still in such pain! It gets worse daily. I know you have healed me many times... my tumor is gone! You have sent the answer to my memory problem, right through my front door, do You not do backs? Is back trouble too hard for You?" I am sorry to say I was not talking very nicely to the Lord; I was speaking as a very frustrated woman in tremendous pain, and totally operating in my flesh. In order to prevent the shocking sensation from traveling up my back and sides, I had spent the last few nights in my lounge chair; I was mentally and physically exhausted.

Keep in mind, I am still flesh; just like everyone else, I experience times of frustration and doubt. This particular Thursday, I was quite upset. While thinking on my dilemma, I answered my own question. "I think not, Lord! So, I must assume, since You have provided me with insurance, You are taking me on this journey for a reason. Maybe there is someone You want me to meet, Lord. I surrender my will." I fervently asked Him to forgive my terrible attitude, and added, "Please don't let me miss Your perfect will. Let our paths cross, and allow me to be a witness to whomever You have chosen!"

Three days later, on Sunday, I sat in the back of the sanctuary in my special chair. It was the final service of a very large conference our church hosts every year. The invitation was given, "If you need prayer for healing, please come forward!" On the platform, several anointed ministers, full of faith, waited expectantly. Many began moving forward, and I watched, as all four isles filled with people in need. The spirit of God has moved in the gift of healing many times in our congregation, and I knew many would receive their miracle. However, I was in such excruciating pain; I did not think I would be able to walk to the front of the sanctuary, so I remained in my chair.

However I noticed another man holding his physically challenged daughter, who remained seated. Since her birth at twenty- six weeks gestation, there had been a steady stream of prayers sent upward on her behalf. Her first year of life was spent in the hospital, where the medical staff held little hope for her survival. With every new obstacle she faced, church members and family, throughout our district, joined together believing God would spare her life.... and He did! Many times throughout that year, during my morning devotions at home, the Lord dealt with me to pray for her. Jesus heard the prayers of His saints and He was making some serious changes in her physical body! The day arrived... Haley finally went home! Eventually they moved to our city and began worshiping with our congregation.

One Sunday morning, during a service two years later, God spoke to me to go to her and pray specifically for her brain. I was completely surprised! I am certainly nothing special; but I know His voice when I hear it and obey. At the altar call, I could not find her; she was not in the sanctuary or the vestibule area. I finally found the Mother holding her child in the fellowship hall. In concern, I asked, "Why are you out here, Baby? It's too chilly for you and Haley to sit here." Her Mother explained the child was fussy; she was afraid they were disrupting the service. I chuckled, "You are in a Pentecostal altar call, and you're "worried" you might make too much noise?"

When I explained the Lord had spoken to me, to pray for Haley, she readily gave me permission to do so. God teaches in His Word for us not ... to pray "amiss". I read in James 4:3 it means be specific, and make sure your motives are pure. Also, to make sure they line up with His word. Of course, I am paraphrasing this. For example, Exodus 20:17 the Ten Commandments teach, "Thou shalt not covet...." Therefore, we wouldn't ask God for someone else's car to be ours, or someone's house to be given to us. I think you get the picture. Feel free to read it for yourself. The Bible is filled with examples of physical healings and miracles; therefore we are not praying "amiss". He endured the stripes on His back to provide healing for us! He instructs us to pray specifically and tell Him exactly what we desire Him to do. So, I placed my hands on each side of her head and I began to pray... "Dear Jesus, I am asking You to heal whatever has been connected wrong. I ask You take it apart and reconnect it right. If there is something in

*there that is not connected at all I ask You to repair it so
this child may have a fuller life. Through all of the
surgeries and sickness you kept her from dying! I know
You did not save her to be as she is, and barely exist;
that is NOT the God I serve! I understand You did not
do this to her, but You are her only hope for healing."
Vehemently, I continued," Dear Jesus, please, heal this
child's brain and let it function correctly! I ask this in
the Name of Jesus; Amen!" I knew if any healing took
place, it had nothing to do with me...JESUS is the
HEALER and He receives ALL of the glory! Afterward,
with a little encouragement, the Mother returned to the
sanctuary with her precious child.*

*When they first began attending church, they
brought Haley in a specially designed stroller. It had a
headrest and apparatus that propped and protected her
from all sides. This precious little darling depended on a
feeding tube around the clock, for she was unable to eat.
She could not focus her eyes; in fact the disability left
her unable to speak, stand, or walk. She did not even
have the muscles to sit upright on her own.*

*Sometimes when I saw them together, I sensed
what her Mother was feeling...so much to the point I
could actually feel a pain in my own heart! Especially,
the times a mournful whine escaped the little girls lips
and I heard the Mama say," What, Baby? Mama doesn't
know what's wrong." I can only imagine the heartache of
a Mother, who wanted so desperately to help her
child...but didn't know how to do it.*

*About two weeks later, after service, she sought
me out. Excitedly, she related, since the Sunday we had
prayed in the fellowship hall, the Lord had touched
Haley; she had made several significant improvements.*

My first reaction was shock! I pray and believe; yet, when I see a miracle, I am completely amazed. It was so exciting to hear words of joy coming from her lips. I questioned, " What kind of changes?" For months, after every service, Cassie, a sweet little girl in our congregation, had made it a point to stop by Haley's stroller and play with her. This ecstatic Mom related her daughter began speaking a few words audibly! One day, suddenly Haley said, " Wanna play with Cassie!" It was MORE than simply a sentence; it showed she now had the ability to form a relationship! Her Mother declared she had done none of this before she was prayed for that Sunday! Overwhelmed with happiness, she added that although the feeding tube was still in place, Haley had begun eating small tastes of soft food without choking, and kept them down. I cannot tell you how excited I was; the joy I felt in my heart at that moment was indescribable! My sweet Jesus had heard ALL the prayers of the saints of God and He answered us!

Throughout the year, along with numerous others, I continued to pray for this precious three year old. Her parents and our church have witnessed miracle after miracle in her life. Haley laughs out loud and speaks more words than we can count! She listens as her Mommy reads to her, and remembers what happens next. Her favorite book is about kittens. She saves the last line to hear her voice say, "And they all cried." It is a beautiful moment, only God could have orchestrated!

Time passed, Haley was now almost four years old, and once again our church was hosting our large annual conference. The altar call was given; when those in need of prayer for healing went forward, I noticed her Father remained seated. She had grown taller and was dead weight to carry, for she had not yet learned the skill of "holding on." I thought to myself, with all of the attached equipment, he must feel unable to stand in line with her for a lengthy period of time. On the other hand, I worried the crowded aisles would block the view, and through no fault of their own, the ministers on the platform would not be able to see them at all.

It was at this moment, the Lord prompted me to approach them and specifically pray for the child's back. In my mind, I immediately recalled Thursday's conversation with the Lord concerning the painful condition of my OWN back. I could not believe He was asking me to pray for hers! However, because I recognized His voice, I rose from my special chair and painfully made my way to the pew. I related my purpose and once again I was granted permission to pray for her. The child set on her Father's lap resting her head upon his shoulder. I spoke a very short prayer. In fact, loudly and with boldness, I spoke the same words I had prayed on Thursday... but with a MUCH different attitude! "Jesus! Do You not do backs? Are backs too hard for You? I think NOT! In the Name of Jesus I command this back to straighten!" As I prayed, I ran my hand up and down her spine, feeling all the lumps and bumps of the curvatures. At that point, my own back condition took over, and I carefully made my way back to my special chair, at the back of the sanctuary. I felt absolutely NOTHING, with the exception of a sad sickening feeling in the pit of my stomach.

Immediately, the enemy began his assault on my mind. "Who do you think you are, to pray something like that?" By the time I reached my seat, I found myself asking the same question. Was I out of my mind? Did

*God truly speak to me to pray for that baby's back?
Again, JESUS is the Healer! No one performs miracles
except HIM! The answer to those questions was not too
long in coming! Two days later, they posted an incredible
picture on "Face Book"! Her Daddy was sitting on the
couch, with his long legs stretched out in front of him.
Haley was standing on the floor between his feet, with
her hands placed on top of his ankles to balance herself!
Rejoicing, I cried out Loud, "Jesus, **did you do it!**"*

*Previously, the doctors had told her family, with
her spine being so crooked, her legs would never be able
to bear the weight of her own body; therefore, she would
never be able to stand. Yet, here I was... looking at an
actual picture of Haley holding on to her Daddy's legs...
not hanging on them... but STANDING and keeping her
balance! What a miracle of God! At that moment, I
began a praise session that lasted off and on until two A.
M. in the morning! I cried like a baby, because once
again, in my heart I KNEW the healing touch of Jesus
was still at work in her body.*

*A few weeks later there "appeared" to be a major
setback. Haley had developed a high fever and began
having convulsions. She was rushed to A.I. DuPont
Children's Hospital in Wilmington, Delaware. That
winter, there were four very contagious viruses
circulating in our state; many children had to be
hospitalized with serious respiratory issues. Somehow,
Haley contacted three of the four all at once! On arrival,
she was unconscious and a breathing tube had already
been inserted by the ambulance crew. From previous
visits, the Emergency Room staff knew of her new found
abilities to eat soft foods and speak; however, not
knowing how long she had been without oxygen,*

before help arrived, they were gravely concerned.

Within a few days, the doctors began weaning her off medications; gradually, she began to wake up. Not knowing if lack of oxygen had damaged her brain, family and hospital staff waited in great anticipation to see if her abilities had been retained or lost. Suddenly, she recognized her Mother's face and clearly uttered the words "Wanna play with Cassie!" Everyone in the room rejoiced and shed tears of joy! It appeared as though none of her functions were lost. Within hours, she was her old self, the virus and fever had subsided; they decided to send her home that very day! However, before she was released, the parents made one more request.

They asked for an x-ray to be made of her spinal column. They explained she had been prayed for, and there was physical evidence that the Lord had straightened their daughter's spine. Keep in mind, at this time the doctors were aware of her eating and speaking, but none of them were aware, that in the time between her prior checkup and this admission...at home, Haley had begun to stand! Very abruptly, he reaffirmed his initial diagnosis... with her severe spinal condition, she would NEVER be able to sit, stand, or walk, and they needed to finally accept this! At that moment, the Father lifted Haley's gown and said, "Look at it! It is straight! Where have all the visible lumps gone?" After the doctors examination, he consented to order an x-ray. Returning to the room, he humbly held his upturned palms outward and said, "What has been done was not by any doctor here at A.I. DuPont Hospital. It was a Higher Being. We see something like this come through here now and then. If she can balance herself here on my table for only five seconds, she will be able to learn to walk!" I can only imagine the parent's excitement, when Haley balanced herself for SIX seconds! The Bible says, Psalms 30:5, "...Weeping may endure for the night, but joy cometh in the morning." They went to the hospital weeping over their sick child and left rejoicing, knowing for certain, GOD had indeed straightened Haley's spine! In addition to her speech and swallowing therapy, she is now receiving physical and aqua therapy. With a specially designed walker, she is able to use her upper body to move forward. This is helping her develop muscles and strengthen her legs. What a God we serve!

God was not finished yet! Haley had an ongoing problem; for months her retinas had been in the process of detaching. Focusing was difficult; in order to see, she turned her head so her eyes would stay still in the corner and not continually "float." The prognosis was not good; eventually, they expected she would lose her sight all together. Each month at home, an eye exam was performed to keep them abreast of her visual digression. The next scheduled appointment occurred the day after her discharge from the hospital. After the examination, the Ophthalmologist asked, "What is going on with your child?" The Mother responded, "Someone prayed and asked God to heal my child's back, and Jesus has straightened her spine!" After providing details of the new x-ray results, the Physician's words, and the fact that Haley had begun standing the Ophthalmologist replied, "That's not all Jesus has done! He has also reattached the retinas in both eyes! You don't need me anymore!" Our Haley no longer turns her head to stop her eyes from "floating". She looks directly at the camera, smiles, and is able to communicate with her family!

I am nothing within myself! However, I have a strong faith and God has given me a boldness to use it. I am not afraid to ask my Heavenly Father for anything; Jesus is the one who answers and heals... all of the praise belongs to Him! Over this span of time, hundreds of people prayed for Haley! I don't care whose prayer it was that touched the throne that day; it could have been anyone. I only care that God answered and His name is glorified!

With the parents signed permission, I have included Haley's journey in this third book. I feel very humbled. First, because God allowed me to personally witness her progression. Secondly, because by any stretch of the educated imagination, my writings skills are far from exceptional! However, I am living proof God does not always call the "qualified". However, if we will answer unafraid, in His time, He WILL qualify the called! My only desire is for Him to continue to use my life as a testimony of His love and power.

~~~~~~~~~~~~~~~~~~~~~~~~~~~~~~~

Since I began this chapter, three years have passed. Haley is enrolled in a special school still receiving Aqua therapy, Physical therapy, and classroom instructions. She has conquered both carpeted and tile floors with her walker. She can move from a lying down to sitting up position all by herself, and then glances around the room with a proud look on her face! The teachers have even motivated her to learn a couple of words in Spanish! Who would have ever thought such a thing possible? Her vocabulary continues to expand, and she loves her sweet treats!

No matter what mountain stands in front of me, I pray He will continue to use me to believe Him for

ANYTHING! I give Him all the praise and glory for what He has done! I have chosen to no longer live "anxiously waiting" for promises to come to pass. I now live "in excited anticipation," knowing they will come to pass Hebrews 10:23 says, "....He is faithful that promised."

Since another year has passed after this story was written; my health insurance was canceled... again, I had to wait ten months to get another policy. I was devastated! How could I ever stand this back pain for that long! But God had other plans. A couple of evenings later, I received a call from a precious friend in Illinois. She felt impressed to pray the prayer of faith for my back. We prayed together over the phone. Two days later, I told Glenn, "Everything looks different to me today! It is strange, but I can't put my finger on exactly why." He smiled at me and replied, "Maybe it is because you are standing up straight!" At this point, for three years, that was impossible; I had to walk in a leaning forward position. It was a great day! It is not perfect, but I am doing so much better I don't know if I will EVER have the surgery. I walk at least a few thousand steps many days a week. Before prayer, that was impossible. I prefer to keep believing and allow Him to complete my healing, Himself. My Jesus can do ANYTHING! He has been so good to me, I cannot tell the half! I thank Him with all my heart. Nothing compares to His greatness that goes on forever!

I Don't Have a Right Not To Tell You

~~~~~~

I have written and shared several stories that I thought may help you along life's path. In some ways, this account is very similar. Not only does my heart want you to be encouraged by these next few pages; I pray you will be enlightened! There is always hope and a loving God, who is forever reaching. He is the answer to whatever you need and like the petals of a rose, He will unfold the beauty before you.

I first met the Lord when I was just an eleven year old child, at a revival service in a little church in New Jersey. I only remember the preacher was a tall blonde lady named Sister Donna. She looked like an angel standing there so tall. She prayed for me and I was so wonderfully overwhelmed with His sweet presence, I wept. It was such a tender encounter of such indescribable peace and love; I was not afraid. It was soon after this, my parents decided we would not be attending this local assembly anymore. Although I had no time to grow spiritually, I never forgot the wonder of His presence. I was twenty- eight, when He entered my life again. Once again, I was so overwhelmed by His spirit I wept. With all the turmoil taking place in my life, I was thrilled in my heart to know, after all these years, Jesus still loved me! I needed Him! My life became so much better; I knew I would never walk away again. That was forty-three years ago and not once have I ever been sorry; I love Him more and more every day.

In the previous narratives of this book, you have already read about the many trials and afflictions I suffered. Jesus delivered me from so many seemingly impossible situations. The desire grew in my heart to begin telling others how He could help them. Of course, the first thing that came to my mind was, "What if they don't understand? Will they think I am crazy? If I began disclosing the deepest recesses of my heart, would they become offended? Could I adequately explain how, the sweet touch of the Spirit made me as happy on the outside, as it did on the inside? Would they think I was boastful?" There were so many questions, to which I had no answers. The truth is, life had left me stripped of any shred of self-esteem. For a long period of time, I had confidence in no one... including myself. I wanted to share the love of Christ, but I faced rejection so many times, I couldn't bear the thought of it happening once again. My wounds were deep; Jesus had just begun the process of restoring my heart. So, as you can see, it was quite an inward battle and I agonized over my decision for a very long time.

The longer I waited, the more I saw God working in my life. I received so many answered prayers; it became even harder to keep this to myself. I was so excited about the transformations taking place inside, I felt like I was going to explode! What was I going to do? Even more so; where should I begin? Was the Lord trying to encourage me to tell others about His love and goodness? I simply wasn't sure, until one day it occurred to me, I didn't have a right not to tell others about my testimony. As I began to share about the love and goodness of Jesus, and tell a little of my personal story, all the doubts melted away!

Others began attending church with me and met the Master the same way I did... at the altar! Not one was disappointed. Of course, there were some who were very happy for me, but felt it was not something they personally needed at this time. Regardless, I continue to share the love of God with my world. Over the years, I wish everyone who started their spiritual journey, continued on... but they didn't. I encouraged all that I could, but ultimately, it was their decision. I love each one dearly and pray one day they will return. Regardless, I know I made the right decision to share my testimony.

This story leads to another incident of great importance; I feel I don't have a right not to tell you about. Once again, I find myself agonizing and wondering if it will be received. Will I offend those who do not believe God could orchestrate such a thing? Will they think less of me, because I believe the Lord sent my answer in a different manner, then what may be considered "normal?" Will it be considered less of a healing because the answer came by information from an acquaintance? If you have read my first two books, you will know the Lord has amazingly healed me many times! He has used various methods, such as medical professionals, nutritionists, physical therapist, and even holistic methods, to nurture my body back to health. He gave physicians the wisdom, knowledge and skill to repair the bodies in many ways. No matter what the source, Jesus, is the Healer! Therefore, I have no right not to share this; I pray it is a blessing to your life.

In my first book, "You Asked God for WHAT?!", I shared my testimony of one particular healing. To keep this compliant with regulations, I will simply say my memory was failing me. This was the demise of both of my parents. Dad's issue came at just fifty-three years of age, and he passed away at seventy. I literally felt as though a piece of my own heart left this earth with him that night! How could something like this happen to such a kind-hearted man, who loved the Lord with all of his heart? A few short years later at seventy, my Mother was stricken with the same issue, and passed away at seventy-seven. Once she gave her heart to the Lord, she became much more loving and kind to everyone. Whatever she could do for her church, family, or friends she did willingly... and always with a smile on her face. If you questioned her motives by asking "Why do you do all the things you do? It was always the same answer; "I do it as unto the Lord!" So I questioned again, "Why this?" "Why now?" I could not understand this at all! My heart was broken.

Among my five siblings, one or more of us visited her in the nursing home daily. However, as she began to severely decline, my two sisters and I sat at her bedside around the clock. Our brothers helped whenever they were able. I always took the overnight shift, from eleven in the evening until seven or eight in the morning. It was very hard... I sat there waiting for every breath. She could no longer speak and make us aware of her pain, but the grimace on her face told the story. As time went on, the nurses and aides became very familiar with us. I had no idea my actions or speech portrayed anything! I was later told, one day after I left to go home, a nurse approached my sister and said, "You do know your sister, Pat, has all the signs of this, too?" My sister answered, "I know, but she doesn't realize it, and I don't know how she would handle it if she did. So, I am not saying anything!" Over a period of weeks, several staff members related their same observances to her. All along, even without being aware of these conversations,

"I" knew I was having issues, but I couldn't bring myself to tell them! I thought I had it well concealed, but found out later, I did not! Apparently, everyone knew it! I never realized that I was repeating things over and over again. What I did realize was at times, just trying to get a sentence out of my mouth was a real struggle; I stumbled over every word in my sentence. Upon entering my kitchen I would find the refrigerator door standing wide open, and think to myself, "Now ,who left that open?" Suddenly, I would realize I was the only one in the house at the time! Many times the water was running full flow into the sink; discovering it, I wondered once more... "Who left that water running?" Again, I was the only one in the house. In conversations, I would stop in the middle of a sentence ,because I had used a word that was completely out of context... like "Butter," when it wasn't even part of the discussion ...they came from nowhere for no reason! I didn't tell my family, but I had already stopped driving with my grandchildren in the car; I didn't want to bring harm to anyone! In fact, the last time I was going to drive I got in my car on a very hot day, with the windows up, and just sat there! I thought, "Whew! It is hot! Why is this car so hot?" Then I realized I was not even in the driver seat, but instead, I was in the passenger seat, and waiting for the car to go! I went back in the house and cried for hours, because I knew I was getting much worse and there would be no more driving!

It was tough for me, because I already knew what was coming. The process of Dad's issue spanned over seventeen years. We helped Mom care for him at home for fourteen years. The final three years, we had no choice but to place him in the local nursing home for around the clock care and medications. Mom's issue came eleven years after Dad's passing. We cared for her at home for three years, and her last three years at the nursing home. Karen, JoAnn, or I, were almost always there. Two of our brothers lived out of state, and the one nearby had a full time job and family to support. Still, they did all they could do to help. Regardless, I knew as a family we had dealt with enough memory problems to last us a lifetime.

Would my reward be to suffer the same thing? I was half angry and half terrified! I couldn't believe this was happening... not after all I had already been through in my life! Would my failing memory rob me of fulfilling my hopes and dreams? I figured my siblings would notice soon enough; I did not have the heart to tell anyone! I refused to even speak its name or admit it to myself out loud. Glenn continually tried his best to reassure me by saying, "Now that things are calming down, you will feel better." With the stress of caregiving eliminated, he was hoping the confusion would disappear. From all I had witnessed, I knew it wouldn't. I felt my life, as I had known it, was over! I continually prayed, "Dear Jesus, will you heal me of this memory problem? I don't understand... please help me, Lord, as only you can!" Without an actual diagnosis, I knew what it was. I could feel myself sinking into this "detached from me" black hole! I sensed it; yet I felt like it was going to be alright. It concerned me, yet it didn't concern me. It was bizarre! I felt like it was someone else, it couldn't be me!

When I expressed my concern to Glenn, he said, "I think it's all the stress you have been through, Honey." It made me feel better, but somehow in my heart I knew *it was more than that!*

I had been through a lot of stress, because his own Mom was in a nursing home fifteen miles in one direction and mine was eight miles the other direction. We went to one, one day, and the other the next. But as they both declined in their health, we went to see both of them each day. So, I would try to appease myself it could be stress.

Looking back, I should have been in complete panic over what was happening to me. I knew where it was taking me, but it concerned me less and less. I was actually very calm. The only way I can describe it is, I existed in a surreal state of mind.

I had good days and bad days; however, the bad days seemed to be increasing. I experienced what I called "floating moments," when it seemed as though my whole body was moving faster than my brain could think. It would frighten me... it was as though I had no control over them. It began about once a month, but after about six months it seemed to happen several times a day. There were no warnings beforehand; I never knew when one would suddenly occur.

During this same time, all of my adult life, I have always had back issues. But for about eight years now, the discomfort would go across my left hip, down the side of my thigh, and on to my shin to the top of my foot! I couldn't find anything to relieve it! I shifted all night long trying to get a place of comfort, but rest would not come. According to the clock on my bed stand, I slept anywhere from five to twelve minutes at a time. On a good night, few and far between, I might sleep for forty minutes. It was awful! The agony brought me to tears... I was nearly crazy with discomfort. Lying down, sitting, or walking, brought no relief. I was exhausted and weary.

My physician ordered a series of ex-rays and an MRI. I was merely fifty-eight at the time, but according to him, I had the back of a ninety- five year old woman! The many injuries from my first marriage had certainly contributed to and sped up the deterioration process. He suggested I should at least try "Percocet", but I instantly declined. I did not want to put anything in my body that could destroy my liver. Nor did I want anything addictive that could destroy my life! My biggest worry was thinking I would end up in a nursing home, like my parents, and be unable to tell them how severe my back discomfort was.

I prayed, "Jesus, please help me find something natural. You know what I'm looking for, and exactly where it is! Please lead me to it, or send it to me!" My prayer was sincere; I knew He had heard me, and in faith believing, I thanked Him for the answer. I have asked and He has helped me so many times; I knew He would not fail me.

For months in my search for something natural to help me, I was introduced to several companies and came in contact with several people, but nothing brought relief. Two days after my prayer, a man I had been introduced to on a three way business conversation, called me. When I answered the phone, the first words he spoke were, "Hey, Pat Gilliss, I have found what you are looking for!" Even though we had never actually met, it seemed as if he had known me for years. He immediately had my attention, for he had certainly not heard my prayer request just two days prior. I knew without a doubt the Lord had sent him to me. I agreed to try a case of his product and in only four days my discomfort was gone! That night, I slept like a baby; I couldn't believe it! I said, "Glenn, I have to remain on this product! I cannot face that horrible misery ever again!" At least one of my discomfort issues was taken care of quickly. I had no idea of the benefit that would come next.

The product itself is not a cure, or does not heal any disease. It merely fired up my own body to heal itself; the way God intended it to, when He designed us.

We were on a fixed income; in order to help me pay for my own product, I began telling others. At the beginning, it was sort of an "ebb and flow" situation, for there were periods my mind was befuddled and my ability to concentrate on the task at hand was limited. It was tried and liked by many of those I love, with several different personal issues. If I could have been able to afford it, I would have given it away...but I couldn't. The best I could do was point them to something that may fire up their own body to heal itself the way it helped mine. It was amazing to hear all the great stories that were pouring in.

After about four and a half months on the product, I suddenly realized my befuddled moments disappeared and my ability to concentrate returned! I had fully returned to my right mind. With my parents, I was told nothing could be done! My husband and family could hardly believe it. One day, in a phone conversation with my sister, Karen, she said," I don't know what that stuff is you are drinking, but it has given me back my sister." Up to this point I was completely unaware I had been repeating specific conversations two or more times in ONE phone call! No one wanted to hurt my feelings, so they just listened over and over again.

Eight years later, I still use this product every day, and still function very well. For years now, I drive and do anything I want to do. In fact, this is my third book based on my past recollections. Not only has it helped my memory issues, my general overall health has greatly improved! My body is fired up and working great!

The stories I have heard from so many others are just amazing. I am thrilled this wonderful man called me and shared it with me. He may not have realized it, but I know without a doubt, God used this man to help save my life! It was a direct answer to my prayer. Had he not led me to this product would I even be here now?

I do NOT have a right not to tell others! I have shared the product with several people, who have faced the same issue I suffered; I recently received a call from the Dallas suburbs. The excited voice on the other end said, "My eighty- six year old Mother has just spoken the first legible sentence she has spoken in six months!" Two months later, she called me again and was so happy to report, her Mother is back to combing her own hair, applies her own makeup, and dresses herself! Even her table manners have returned. Hearing this, there is only one way I can explain the feelings in my heart. Yes! I felt like a million bucks!

Should you choose to try this product, you can visit my web site at www.youaskedgodforwhat.com *and fill out the three minute survey.* **I will personally** *get back to you. I will be the only one to read your survey. I don't have a right not to share it! How do you know that He did not send it to YOU through this book, in answer to your prayers? I know He sent it to me! I thank Him every day for this blessing!*

Yes, I am sure there will be naysayers, yet if one person is helped it will be worth it to take the time to write this story. Just like my personal testimony about Christ, I will continue sifting and sorting. By word of mouth, I will wholeheartedly share my wonderful experience with this product. In Jesus name, I pray you are blessed!

Such a difference has been made in so many lives, not only by my testimony, but the words of many others. If you try this product, to help your own body fire up and heal itself, how many more could be encouraged and helped by your testimony? We don't have a right NOT TO TELL THEM, do we?

Chuckles Corner
Brendon and the Mac and Cheese
~~~~~~~~~~~~~~~~~~~~~~~~~~~~~~~~~~

I thought I would end this book with a couple of humorous stories, to make someone smile. I hope you laugh out loud!

Our precious three year old Grandson, Brendon, was eating dinner with his family. My daughter, Amy, noticed he was not eating his favorite macaroni and cheese. She said, "Brendon, you haven't touched your mac and cheese." His reply was, "I don't like it." She continued, "But Brendon that is your favorite food! You have always loved your mac and cheese." He answered her again, "No, it will make me sick, and I'll die! I can't eat it!" She said he was so serious she didn't know what to think. His Daddy decided to show him it would be okay to eat and took a fork and took a bite, himself. Brendon said nothing! He just sat in total silence staring at his Daddy. So, Tim decided to make a real scene. As a joke, he grabbed himself by the throat, coughing and gagging. Finally, he dropped out of his chair and hit the floor in total silence! He laid there, as dead, waiting for a reaction from this three-year old, who watching in absolute silence. Finally, Brendon peered over the table at Tim and boldly said, "TOLD YA!" needless to say Brendon and the entire family had a huge laugh!

Chuckles Corner
Easter Play Through the Eyes of a Child
~~~~~~~~~~~~~~~~~~~~~~~~~~~~~~~~~~~~~~~

For several years, our local assembly performed a huge Easter drama, called "Messiah". This particular year; I did not participate, along with my two older children, in order to take care of our twins. Glenn played the part of John the Baptist. Andy knelt beside me in the pew and played with his little figures. He had no interest in the play, but he was content. However, Ashley perched on my lap and intently watched the performance. We were right next to the center aisle, with a wonderful view.

Once the scenes came closer to the crucifixion and the play became more dramatic, Ashley asked me very quietly, "What are they doing now, Mommy?" I said, "They are bringing Jesus before Pilate." Her response was, "OOH!" The next scene came, and again she whispered, "What are they doing now, Mommy?" I said, "They are taking Jesus to Calvary." "OHHH," she said. Yet again, during the next scene, she whispered, "What are they doing now, Mommy?" I responded gently, "They are hanging Him on the cross, Baby." She became very quiet. At this point, she seemed to be quite content, at least for the moment.

At the end of the play, it was time for Jesus to resurrect from the tomb. The music got louder and victorious! They began fogging the sanctuary with dry ice to surround the tomb. Through the cloud, it was hard to see, and Jesus was going to come out of the tomb at any second! As the music became even MORE intense; before I could stop her, my little darling

151

screamed out, "Are they going to cook Him and eat Him!?" I grabbed her mouth trying to quiet her, but it was no use, everyone within a ten-foot radius was laughing their heads off. I could have died in my seat, except ...I was laughing too hard myself! It was so embarrassing at the time! Looking back now, it was funny! Not very timely, but none-the-less hilarious! Writing this, I laughed again. I don't think I shall ever forget it.

Epilogue

~~~~~~

As you have read this book, I am certain many of you have been able to relate to at least some of what has happened in my life. Perhaps, you can identify with several situations or even all of them. I did not write this book to look for any sympathy, but my desire was to enlighten you. Jesus is waiting to help you, just as He did me. I want you to realize you are not alone. There are many others whose stories are much like my own and even worse, who have overcome by the power of His blood. Up to this point, if your life has seemed like nothing but a disaster... it doesn't have to stay that way! You can find GOD! Whether you breathe His name in a whisper, or cry out in desperation, He will hear and help you.

I now live a very full and happy life. God's goodness has renewed my faith, and His comfort bound my wounds and healed my scars. I have opened my heart to trust again. I am currently able to let more people in my circle of life. Once again, my heart is filled with love, enjoyment and understanding ...and yes, even compassion and forgiveness, to all that may have hurt me, whether it was knowingly or unaware. I no longer have to look over my shoulder in fear; for God has given me the courage to face anything! When I had no faith of my own, He taught me how to walk by faith in Him. Because I have come to truly know Him as my "Heavenly Father," and I am beginning to comprehend just how much He loves me, I am not afraid to ask Him for anything. God has blessed me with the greatest husband on earth and four wonderful children.

My children are all happily married to wonderful spouses and work for the Lord the best they know how. In addition, the Lord graced our lives with the addition of eleven grandchildren. In fact, we just learned we have a "Great" grandchild on the way!

I guess what I am trying to convey is, as my Pastor once said, "Jesus can turn a mess into a message." If God can turn my life around, then He can certainly take care of yours! I pray you develop a deeper relationship with the Master; allow Him to guide you and fill your life with blessings, too.

As for all of you precious saints of God, who have faithfully followed Him for years, I know you will continue to reach for the lost and lonely. Your Christ-like love will show them the way to HIM!

I sincerely thank you all for reading my books. May God bless. I pray you are blessed by His kind and loving hands forever. In Jesus Name-Amen....

Final Notes;

    This is Pat Gilliss, "Author of the Other Side of Broken" There is a short three minute survey, if you are interested in the product. I am the only one who will see your answers to this survey and will be the only one responding personally to you. I hope to meet you soon. Please go to this domain to inquire.
www.youaskedgodforwhat.com

12886874R00099

Made in the USA
Middletown, DE
16 November 2018